TOUR OF MONT BLANC

About the Author

Kev Reynolds is a freelance writer and lecturer, and a prolific author of guidebooks, whose first title for Cicerone (*Walks and Climbs in the Pyrenees*) appeared in 1978, and is still in print. He has written numerous books on the Alps, a series of trekkers' guides to Nepal and, nearer to home, several that focus on walking in southern England. A collection of short stories harvested from his 50 years among mountains (*A Walk in the Clouds*), was published by Cicerone in 2013, and his memoir recounting eight trekking expeditions in the Nepal Himalaya appeared in 2015, with the title *Abode of the Gods*.

Elected an honorary member of the Outdoor Writers' & Photographers' Guild, SELVA (the Société d'Etudes de la Littérature de Voyage Anglophone), and the British Association of International Mountain Leaders (BAIML), Kev is also a member of the Alpine Club and the Austrian Alpine Club. His enthusiasm for the countryside in general, and mountains in particular, remains undiminished after a lifetime's activity, and during the winter months he regularly travels throughout Britain to share that enthusiasm through his lectures.

Check him out on www.kevreynolds.co.uk.

Other Cicerone titles by the author

100 Hut Walks in the Alps

Abode of the Gods

Alpine Pass Route

A Walk in the Clouds

Chamonix to Zermatt

Everest: a Trekker's Guide

The Bernese Oberland

The Cotswold Way

The North Downs Way

The Pyrenees

The South Downs Way

Tour of the Jungfrau Region

Tour of the Oisans: The GR54

Tour of the Vanoise

Trekking in the Alps

Trekking in the Himalaya

Trekking in the Silvretta & Rätikon Alps

Walking in Austria

Walking in Kent

Walking in Sussex

Walking in the Alps

Walking in the Valais

Walks and Climbs in the Pyrenees

Walks in the Engadine

Walks in the South Downs National Park

TOUR OF MONT BLANC

by
Kev Reynolds

JUNIPER HOUSE, MURLEY MOSS,
OXENHOLME ROAD, KENDAL, CUMBRIA LA9 7RL
www.cicerone.co.uk

© Kev Reynolds 2015
Fourth edition 2015
ISBN: 978 1 85284 779 1
Reprinted 2016 (with updates), 2017 (with updates)
Third edition 2011
Second edition 2007
First edition 2002

A catalogue record for this book is available from the British Library.
All photographs are by the author unless otherwise stated.
Printed in China on behalf of Latitude Press Ltd.

 The routes of the GR®, PR® and GRP® paths in this guide have been reproduced with the permission of the Fédération Française de la Randonnée Pédestre holder of the exclusive rights of the routes. The names GR®, PR® and GRP® are registered trademarks. © FFRP 2015 for all GR®, PR® and GRP® paths appearing in this work.

Dedication

This book is dedicated to the memory of Andrew Harper
(1930–2001), author of the first English-language guide to the
Tour of Mont Blanc.

Updates to this Guide

While every effort is made by our authors to ensure the accuracy of guidebooks as they go to print, changes can occur during the lifetime of an edition. Any updates that we know of for this guide will be on the Cicerone website (www.cicerone.co.uk/779/updates), so please check before planning your trip. We also advise that you check information about such things as transport, accommodation and shops locally. Even rights of way can be altered over time. We are always grateful for information about any discrepancies between a guidebook and the facts on the ground, sent by email to updates@cicerone.co.uk or by post to Cicerone, Juniper House, Murley Moss, Oxenholme Road, Kendal LA9 7RL, United Kingdom.

Register your book: To sign up to receive free updates, special offers and GPX files where available, register your book at www.cicerone.co.uk.

Front cover: Mont Blanc from the Grand Balcon Sud between La Flégère and Le Brévent

CONTENTS

Key to Route Profiles

⌂   accommodation: mountain hut, hotel, dortoir, gite...

△   official campsite

♈   refreshments: food, and/or drinks

🚌 bus service   🚃 railway station

🚡   mechanical lift: cable-car, gondola, chairlift etc

Mountain Safety

Every mountain walk has its dangers, and those described in this guidebook are no exception. All who walk or climb in the mountains should recognise this and take responsibility for themselves and their companions along the way. The author and publisher have made every effort to ensure that the information contained herein was correct when the guide went to press, but they cannot accept responsibility for any loss, injury or inconvenience sustained by any person using this book.

International Distress Signal *(emergency only)*
Six blasts on a whistle (and flashes with a torch after dark) spaced evenly for one minute, followed by a minute's pause. Repeat until an answer is received. The response is three signals per minute followed by a minute's pause. The following signals are used to communicate with a helicopter:

Help required
Raise both arms above head to form a 'Y'

Help not required
Raise one arm above head and extend the other downward, to form the diagonal of an 'N'

Emergency telephone numbers
For general emergencies –112
For mountain rescue in Italy –118;
in Switzerland helicopter rescue (REGA) can be summoned via 1414

Weather reports
(If telephoning from the UK the dialling codes are:
France: 0033; Italy: 0039; Switzerland: 0041)

France: Chamonix: tel 08 92 68 02 74, www.meteo.fr or tel 3250
Italy: tel 0165 44 113
Switzerland: 162 (in French, German or Italian),
www.meteoschweiz.ch/en

Note Mountain rescue can be very expensive – be adequately insured.

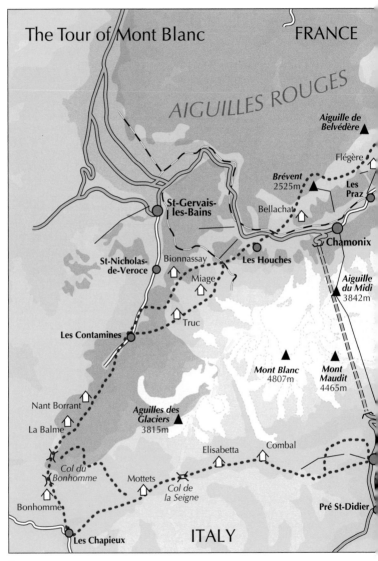

The Tour of Mont Blanc — FRANCE

AIGUILLES ROUGES

Aiguille de Belvédère ▲

Flégère

Brévent 2525m ▲

Les Praz

St-Gervais-les-Bains

Bellachat

Chamonix

St-Nicholas-de-Veroce

Bionnassay

Les Houches

Miage

Aiguille du Midi ▲ 3842m

Truc

Les Contaimes

▲ **Mont Blanc** 4807m

▲ **Mont Maudit** 4465m

Nant Borrant

La Balme

Aguilles des Glaciers ▲ 3815m

Elisabetta

Combal

Col du Bonhomme

Mottets

Col de la Seigne

Bonhomme

Pré St-Didier

Les Chapieux

ITALY

On the path from the Col de la Seigne to Rifugio Elisabetta

INTRODUCTION

Were it to stand alone with no near neighbour to lend it scale, the great snow- and ice-crusted dome of Mont Blanc would still lay claim to the title of Monarch of the Alps. At 4807m (15,771ft) the summit stands a good 3700m (12,000ft) above Chamonix, and is 3km higher than the nearest habitation on the Italian flank. On blue-sky days it dazzles in the sunshine or floats on a raft of cloud, commanding one's attention with its dominating height, for it has a regal presence equal both to its appearance and its stature. That presence is not always benign, of course, for the mountain also dictates the weather and controls the climate of its surrounding valleys. But catch it in a benevolent mood, and those valleys bask in its glory.

Mont Blanc does not stand alone, however, and the large number of attendant peaks and aiguilles, savage rock walls, ridges and tumbling glaciers, rather than detract from its grandeur, simply add to it with their own individuality – courtiers whose impressive company would grace any massif anywhere in the world. The Grandes Jorasses, Aiguille Noire, the Verte and Drus, Aiguille du Midi, Mont Maudit and Mont Dolent, on which the borders of three countries meet, each of these (and there are many more) would stand out in any mountain crowd. Here they attend court, subdued only by altitude.

The summit of Le Brévent rewards with a direct view of Mont Blanc across the valley

Mont Blanc then is more than just the highest mountain in Europe west of the Caucasus. Indeed, it's more than a big mountain massif, it's a mountain range, compact and complete in itself. According to Roger Frison-Roche, this beautiful 25km-long wall of rock, snow and ice has some 400 summits and more than 40 glaciers that scour the heartland and add lustre to every scene. Carrying the frontiers of three countries, France, Italy and Switzerland, it is moated by seven valleys – those of the Arve, Montjoie, des Glaciers, Veni, the two Vals Ferret (one Italian, the other Swiss), and the Vallée du Trient – valleys that define the limits of the range, and through which winds the route of the Tour of Mont Blanc (TMB), a trekker's route that revels in some of the most exquisite mountain scenery of all.

THE TOUR OF MONT BLANC

Over a period of 10 to 12 days the TMB entices walkers on a circuit of this magnificent mountain block, making a journey of around 170km (105 miles), with an accumulated height gain and loss of something like 10,000m (32,800ft). Depending on the precise route taken (for there are variations), there are 10 or 11 passes to cross as the tour progresses from one valley to the next. Each of these valleys enjoys unforgettable views, and each has its own individual character – the bustling, tourist-centred Vallée de l'Arve (the Chamonix

valley), the sparsely inhabited Vallée des Glaciers, the pastoral Swiss Val Ferret, to name but three.

That the TMB is the most popular long walk in Europe is not in doubt. In excess of 10,000 people embark on this circuit each summer. Why? Well, everyone's heard of Mont Blanc, and anyone with more than a passing interest in mountains will know of its stunning scenery. Beyond this, the TMB's reputation as one of the great walks of the world has long been established. Longer, in fact, than any other alpine route.

The first pedestrian tour around Mont Blanc took place as long ago as 1767, when Horace Bénédict de Saussure and friends set out from Chamonix with an entourage of guides, porters and mules to explore the range by way of the Col du Bonhomme, Col de la Seigne, Courmayeur and the Grand St Bernard Pass. Saussure was imbued with a love of mountains in general and Mont Blanc in particular, and in all he made three full tours of the range, sleeping in beds where available, but otherwise accepting with equanimity the hay of a simple alp hut or chalet. As a scientist he travelled to expand his knowledge of the range and its structure, taking time to meditate on the geology, but also to eulogize its beauty.

Sixty years later JD Forbes, the Professor of Natural Philosophy at Edinburgh, succeeded Saussure by combining scientific observation with

As on so much of the TMB the scenery on the trail from Col de Balme to Col des Posettes is spectacular

a true love of mountains, and made his own tour of Mont Blanc in 1839, concluding that 'the most successful of Alpine travellers will, if disposed to be candid, admit that the happiest, if not the proudest, moments of their experiences, had been spent on some of the more majestic passes of the Alps, or on some summits not of the highest class.'

Such sentiments have since been shared by many tens of thousands who have followed in his footsteps.

The TMB became increasingly popular during the mid-Victorian age, when it was almost invariably experienced on the back of a mule, but the growth of outdoor activities in the 20th century established the route as

the ultimate long mountain walk. And it's not hard to see why.

THE ROUTE

Being a circular route, the Tour of Mont Blanc could be walked in either a clockwise or an anti-clockwise direction, and started from any one of a number of places. By tradition it has begun in the Chamonix valley (the Vallée de l'Arve), but not in Chamonix itself, for in order to make the most of the splendid views afforded of Mont Blanc from the slopes of the Aiguilles Rouges chain, the route avoids the bed of the valley except to cross it at either end. Instead, by tradition the TMB begins about 7km downvalley from Chamonix, in Les Houches, and tackles the circuit in an anti-clockwise direction.

From here the way climbs to Col de Voza, then divides. One option descends on the far side to Bionnassay, Le Champel and Les Contamines in the Val Montjoie which cuts along the western edge of the Mont Blanc range. The other, and more challenging, option goes up the slope towards the Bionnassay glacier, then descends below its snout before climbing to Col de Tricot, dropping to the delightful Chalets de Miage, then climbing again to cross a shoulder of Mont Truc before descending at last to Les Contamines, where the two routes coincide.

An hour's gentle valley stroll leads to the celebrated church of Notre-Dame de la Gorge, beside which a paved mule path dating from Roman times rises into a lovely hanging valley that grows wilder as height is gained towards Col du Bonhomme, which in turn directs the route up another 150m to the Col de la Croix du Bonhomme at 2483m (8146ft). On the south side of the saddle stands a large refuge owned by the CAF (Club Alpin Français), enjoying fine views to Mont Pourri and the Tarentaise mountains.

The continuing route of the TMB descends to the Vallée des Glaciers, but here again there are two ways of achieving this. The most direct goes straight down below the refuge to join the valley at the hamlet of Les Chapieux, while the alternative cuts left at the Col de la Croix and heads

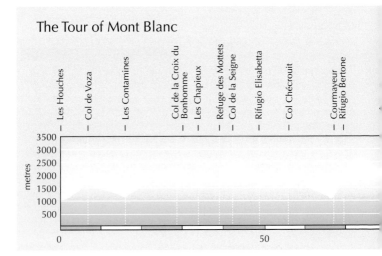

The Tour of Mont Blanc

Dolonne, with the Dent du Géant, Rochefort Arête and Grandes Jorasses as a formidable backdrop

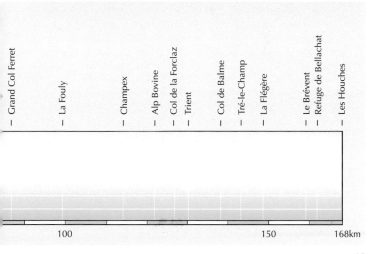

– Grand Col Ferret	– La Fouly	– Champex	– Alp Bovine	– Col de la Forclaz	– Trient	– Col de Balme	– Tré-le-Champ	– La Flégère	– Le Brévent / – Refuge de Bellachat	– Les Houches

100   150   168km

up to the barren Col des Fours, from which a surprise view is gained of Mont Blanc peering above a distant ridge linking the Trélatête with Aiguille des Glaciers. Descent from Col des Fours is by way of a steep slope of scree and pasture leading to farm buildings at the Ville des Glaciers, some way upvalley beyond Les Chapieux. A short walk up a track from here brings you to the Refuge des Mottets, ideally situated at the foot of the climb to Col de la Seigne.

The 2516m (8255ft) saddle of Col de la Seigne is at once the gateway into Italy and a magnificent viewpoint. Mont Blanc is seen to advantage from here, set off as it is by the contrast of a deep sweeping valley, the limestone slabs of the Pyramides Calcaire and a long view which shows the Italian flank of the range in sharp profile. It's one of the finest panoramas of the whole walk, and one to absorb at leisure.

When at last you tear yourself away, a path descends gently across pastures into the Vallon de la Lée Blanche, in effect the upper reaches of Val Veni, which cuts directly below the mountains' feet. Before reaching the valley bed, however, Rifugio Elisabetta is seen off to the left, backed by the Trélatête and Glacier de la Lée Blanche that cascades behind the hut. Easy walking brings the TMB down to Lac Combal and the huge moraine wall of the Miage glacier, then the path swings to the right and makes a long ascent of hillside which directs

the route to the ski slopes of Col Chécrouit. Until these are reached, this stage of the trek is quite simply magnificent. Step by step the route parallels the south side of the Mont Blanc range with views of indescribable beauty, sometimes doubled and inverted by reflection in a wayside pool. In fact the walk from Col de la Seigne to Col Chécrouit would alone make the TMB worth tackling.

At the col the way forks once more. The direct route to Courmayeur descends via the crowded but attractive village of Dolonne, while the alternative option cuts down into the Val Veni opposite the Brenva glacier, then curves round the base of Mont Chétif for a final road walk into town.

Courmayeur is to the Italian side of Mont Blanc what Chamonix is to the French, but it's much smaller and better contained than its counterpart on the other side of the mountain, has long been known for its mineral springs and today enjoys an atmosphere conducive to relaxation. Should you feel in need of a day's rest, Courmayeur is the place for it.

Yet again the TMB walker is faced with a choice of routes. Above Rifugio Bertone, the main TMB has been routed along the bewitchingly scenic north flank of Mont de la Saxe to Rifugio Bonatti, while its former course – a more demanding one now used as a *variante* – continues steeply uphill to gain the Mont de la Saxe ridge, famed as a belvedere from which to study the Grandes Jorasses

Looking down on Rifugio Bertone and back to Mont Chétif from the Mont de la Saxe route. Courmayeur is in the valley

across the depths of Val Ferret. At the end of this ridge Col Sapin lies at the head of the little Val Sapin through which a bad-weather alternative route rises from Courmayeur. From the col the two *variantes* cross the head of the Armina glen, then climb to Pas Entre-Deux-Sauts at 2524m (8281ft) which gives access to the pastoral Vallon de Malatra, and there join the main route at the Bonatti hut, named after the celebrated Italian mountaineer. From here the way remains high above the Val Ferret on another gloriously scenic path, only descending to the bed of the valley just below Rifugio Elena which lies at its head.

Above the Elena refuge the tour crosses into Switzerland at the Col du Grand Ferret (2537m, 8323ft),

then slopes down across a succession of pastures to the Swiss Val Ferret, a gentle valley that marks the eastern extent of the Mont Blanc range. There are several small villages and hamlets of timber and stone buildings strung along the valley, and the TMB visits most of them. Apart from a beautiful section between the dairy farm of La Peule, and the hamlet of Ferret, the route stays low, gaining snatches of views rather than the more open vistas of the Italian flank, yet it's a very pleasant walk all the same, with plenty of variety to maintain one's interest.

Towards the northern end of the valley the path climbs through forest and emerges at the lakeside resort of Champex, from where backward views are dominated by the Grand

17

Combin. Out of Champex the route divides once more. The generally accepted main route passes through the hamlets of Champex d'en Haut and Champex d'en Bas, then follows an undulating course in and out of woodland and over high pastureland to the Bovine alp (with views into the Rhône valley) before reaching the road pass of Col de la Forclaz overlooking the Vallée du Trient and the village from which it takes its name.

The alternative to the Bovine route is a tough but rewarding crossing of the steep and rocky Fenêtre d'Arpette, which at 2665m (8743ft) shares with Col des Fours (the alternative route to the Vallée des Glaciers) the honour of being the highest point on the Tour of Mont Blanc. The Fenêtre provides a sudden, spectacular view as you emerge through a narrow gap to be confronted by the icefall of the Trient glacier just ahead. The way then leads down alongside the glacier to a path which accompanies a *bisse*, or irrigation channel, but with another option to consider. The bisse path contours along the hillside to the Col de la Forclaz, where it meets the Bovine option, while a second route crosses the glacial torrent on a footbridge, then faces yet another choice. Either continue downvalley to Trient, or bear left and climb the western hillside to Refuge Les Grands.

Col de Balme on the Franco-Swiss border is the next place to aim for. One route climbs to the pass from Trient through a little valley drained by the Nant Noir stream, the other tackles a steeply sloping hillside above Refuge Les Grands, the two routes joining at the refuge on the summit of the pass. Col de Balme reintroduces TMB walkers to France and the Vallée de l'Arve spread out below. A broad path swings down the slope to Le Tour at the head of the valley, but another and more scenic trail goes along the crest of the Aiguillette des Posettes before dropping steeply to the hamlet of Tré-le-Champ.

On leaving Tré-le-Champ the TMB climbs at first through forest, then over more open and rocky ground within the Réserve Naturelle des Aiguilles Rouges. Reaching the base of the Aiguillette d'Argentière, the way ascends a series of metal ladders, rungs and handrails fixed against abrupt rock walls – definitely not for the faint-hearted! Fortunately an easier alternative is provided on a path that enters the nature reserve at Col des Montets, and the two routes amalgamate at the top of the ladder route where a huge cairn stands at a junction of paths looking across to the Mer de Glace and along the chain of mountains to Mont Blanc.

The onward route eases along the hillside 1000m or more above the valley, passing below a fine waterfall and eventually reaching the Refuge La Flégère set beside a cableway that rises from Les Praz de Chamonix. Across the valley the ice river of the Mer de Glace directs your gaze past the Aiguille Verte and Drus to the big

The Col du Brévent, where the GR5 meets the TMB

wall of the Grandes Jorasses, a stunning view that ensures a night spent at La Flégère will be truly memorable. An alternative trail visits the higher Refuge du Lac Blanc and the justifiably famous tarn beside it.

The final stage of the Mont Blanc circuit is a constant adoration of the Monarch of the Alps as the way continues high above the valley, crosses the hillside to the ski area of Plan Praz, then goes up a winding trail to Col de Brévent, where you may be lucky to catch sight of the elusive bouquetin, or ibex, followed by an undemanding climb to the summit of Le Brévent itself. The 2526m (8287ft) crown of this mountain was acknowledged more than two centuries ago as presenting an unrivalled view of Mont Blanc, and it's fitting that the TMB should come here on the final day. A simple restaurant on the very summit provides ample excuse to sit with a cool drink to enjoy that wonderful panorama and reflect on the journey that has brought you this far, before making the steep and knee-trembling descent all the way to the valley bed 1500m (4900ft) below, then up to Les Houches, where the long walk began.

Or, of course, you could tackle the route in a clockwise direction.

CLOCKWISE OR ANTI-CLOCKWISE?

Although the route is now well established as an anti-clockwise circuit, there are arguments in favour of

19

walking the TMB in a clockwise direction, the most persuasive being that by travelling 'against the flow' one meets different people at each night's rest, while during the first hour or two of the walking day the path is virtually empty, then comes a wave of trekkers followed by another period of calm. On the other hand, when following the anti-clockwise trend there are nearly always other walkers in view. This can be either comforting or distracting, depending on your outlook.

As for the steepness or otherwise of ascents and descents, there's little to choose between the two options.

The first English-language guide to the Tour of Mont Blanc was written by the late Andrew Harper, who naturally described the route in the traditional anti-clockwise direction. The four editions of his guide deservedly sold in large numbers and thereby encouraged tens of thousands of English-speaking mountain walkers to follow his preferred circuit. But having walked the TMB in both directions, and seen at first hand the merits of both options, the present guidebook contains directions for anti-clockwise and clockwise routings. After all, the Tour of Mont Blanc makes such a splendid two-week holiday that there are bound to be readers who, having walked it once, will dream of doing it again. This book, hopefully, will entice you to do just that, but in a different direction!

However, if tackling the TMB as a clockwise circuit, it is not advisable to begin at the traditional starting point of Les Houches, for being faced with the very steep 1500m ascent to Le Brévent on the very first day would be enough to intimidate most recreational walkers. It would be better to start at Champex in order to be mountain-fit before the first of the challenging ascents appears. Details of how to reach the start of the walk – whichever direction you choose – will be found below. Argentière is an alternative starting-point. The walking is more immediately harder, but access may be easier.

SUGGESTED ITINERARIES

The following itineraries are suggestions only, but their inclusion may help at the initial planning stage. Thanks to the number and diverse nature of accommodation facilities that exist throughout the route, it is perfectly feasible to vary these proposals as time, weather and fitness dictate. Details are given within this guide wherever accommodation is to be found, and this information should enable you to vary the staging of your walk to suit, for your own experience of mountain walking may well demand a very different itinerary.

Traditional (anti-clockwise) circuit: 11 days

1 Les Houches – Les Contamines
2 Les Contamines – Les Chapieux
3 Les Chapieux – Rifugio Elisabetta
4 Rifugio Elisabetta – Courmayeur
5 Courmayeur – Rifugio Bonatti

The Tré-la-Tête (left) and Glacier du Miage mirrored in a pool high above Val Veni

6   Rifugio Bonatti – La Fouly
7   La Fouly – Champex
8   Champex – Col de la Forclaz/
    Trient
9   Col de la Forclaz/Trient
    – Tré-le-Champ
10 Tré-le-Champ – La Flégère
11 La Flégère – Les Houches

Clockwise circuit: 10 days
1   Champex – La Léchère/Ferret
2   La Léchère/Ferret – Rifugio
    Bonatti
3   Rifugio Bonatti – Courmayeur
4   Courmayeur – Rifugio Elisabetta
5   Rifugio Elisabetta – Refuge de la
    Croix du Bonhomme
6   Refuge de la Croix du
    Bonhomme – Les Contamines

7   Les Contamines – Les Houches
8   Les Houches – La Flégère
9   La Flégère – Trient
10 Trient – Champex

HOW TO GET THERE

By air to Geneva, then by bus to Les Houches and Chamonix

Scheduled flights from the UK to Geneva are operated by British Airways (www.britishairways.com), Swiss International Airways (www. swiss.com) and EasyJet (www.easyjet. com). Aer Lingus (www.aerlingus.ie) flies from Dublin.

British Airways fly from London Heathrow and Gatwick, Birmingham and Manchester. Swiss International uses London Heathrow and City. EasyJet operates out of Gatwick, Luton, East Midlands and Liverpool.

Flights to Geneva from the USA – New York, Chicago, Los Angeles and Miami – are by Continental, United Airlines and/or Lufthansa.

At the time of writing, seasonal twice-daily buses operated by SAT Autocar offer an effective link between Geneva Airport and Chamonix; the journey takes around two hours with a scheduled drop-off at Les Houches. Timetables can be accessed on www.gare-routiere. com and it's also possible to book tickets online. By this method you're given a reservation number which you quote on collecting tickets at the Gare Routière information desk in the main hall at Geneva Airport. Or check details of the private transfer company, Mountain Drop Offs, www.mountain dropoffs.com.

By air to Geneva followed by train to Les Houches or Chamonix

Should your arrival at Geneva Airport be too late to connect with the bus to Les Houches/Chamonix, try the train. From the airport take a train to Cornavin station; then catch tram no.16 to the stop known as Amandolier SNCF. A three-minute walk leads to the Gare des Eaux-Vives from where trains depart for St Gervais (possible change at Les Roches sur Foron). From St Gervais take the local train to Les Houches or Chamonix.

By air to Geneva, followed by train and bus to Martigny, Orsières and Champex

The Geneva–Champex journey is useful for walkers tackling the TMB in a clockwise direction. Travel by air to Geneva as detailed above, then by train from Geneva Airport to Martigny, where you change to the St Bernard Express. This colourful local train is taken as far as Orsières, followed by Postbus to Champex.

By train to Les Houches and Chamonix via St Gervais

Travel by rail from the UK is straightforward, with a high-speed London–Paris link via Eurostar (www.eurostar.com) through the Channel Tunnel. St Gervais, downvalley from Chamonix, is served by trains on the main French railway network (SNCF), with at least two departures per day from Paris Gare de Lyon. The onward journey to Les Houches and Chamonix is by local train.

By train via Lausanne to Martigny and Chamonix

The super-fast TGV network has a useful route from Paris to Lausanne (Switzerland). Lausanne connects with the Geneva–Martigny service referred to in paragraph 3 above. Walkers planning to start their TMB at Les Houches must change trains in Martigny and take the Mont Blanc Express to Chamonix. This train involves a change (simply cross from one platform to the next) at Le

The unpretentious village of Trient is a major staging post on the TMB

Châtelard on the Swiss/French border. From Chamonix either change for a local train to Les Houches, or take a ten-minute bus ride – buses leave from the railway station.

WHEN TO GO

The season for high-level walking in the Alps is dictated by the amount and timing of the previous winter's snowfall, and restrictions imposed by the onset of cold, inclement weather of the autumn. Since the TMB trekker has to negotiate several passes where avalanche could be a distinct possibility if attempted too soon, the end of June or first week in July is probably the earliest time to start. By then paths are largely snow-free and mountain flowers adding their riot of colour to the meadows. Of course, there may be some years when it is safe to set out at the beginning of June, while it's not unknown to have a heavy dump of snow in the middle of August. The only certainty when it comes to predicting alpine weather is that any long-range forecast is bound to be unpredictable!

The peak summer holiday period in France usually falls between 15 July and the end of August, and one may expect the route to be at its busiest at this time. Note that at the end of August the 'Ultra Trail' mountain marathon takes place when around 2500 competitors run non-stop around the TMB. Should you plan to tackle the TMB between these dates, you are strongly advised to telephone ahead to reserve overnight accommodation.

Often the best (most settled) weather comes in the first half of September, but on occasion an 'Indian Summer' spreads throughout the month and well into October. On the other hand, if the weather deteriorates some facilities are likely to close early. October can be a magical month in the Alps, with crisp night frosts and bright days with the first snows dusting the higher passes. It's then possible to walk the TMB in glorious solitude, although overnight accommodation may not be easy to find. Refuges will almost certainly be closed, but a winter room may be accessible.

To summarise: the safest time (weather and accommodation-wise) to attempt the Tour of Mont Blanc is from early July to mid-September.

ACCOMMODATION

There's no shortage of accommodation along the route, and this appears to grow in number and variety almost year by year. This accommodation is not confined to centres of habitation, and some of the most remarkable lodgings will be found in seemingly remote locations. It may be true to say that the places you stay overnight will in due course count among the most memorable features of your tour.

Outline details, including websites and telephone numbers, are given in this book where lodgings exist. Advance booking is essential for most refuges, and highly recommended for other forms of accommodation. The following website lists all refuges and gîtes

The gîte Le Moulin offers welcome accommodation below Tré-le-Champ

Rifugio Elisabetta, backed by the Tré-la-Tête

along the route of the TMB, and provides a facility to reserve beds and meal in advance – a deposit via credit card is required by most lodgings. See www.autourdumontblanc.com.

Prices are not quoted in this guide, but as an indication of costs likely to be incurred, comparisons with UK prices are very favourable. Bed and breakfast in modest **hotels** used during research were of a similar price to that of British B&Bs, and a filling evening meal in a French, Italian or Swiss restaurant along the route would be equal in price to a pub meal in the UK. Half-pension (*demi-pension*) usually provides the most economical deal. Some hotels have dormitory rooms (*dortoirs*) as well as standard bedrooms and these offer a cheaper option.

Dortoirs are to be found in a number of locations and are recommended for those walkers who do not object to a lack of privacy. Apart from the few hotels referred to above which offer dormitory accommodation, there are also **gîtes d'étape**, which may be likened to privately run youth hostels. These gîtes provide showers, communal sleeping quarters, a full meals service (usually) and, in some instances, self-catering facilities. All of those used during research gave good value for money.

Few of the **mountain huts** (*refuges/rifugios*) on the TMB are owned by member groups of the French, Italian or Swiss Alpine Clubs; most are in private ownership but open to all. Here again mixed-sex dormitory accommodation is the norm.

Clothes washing on the Tour

The majority of TMB refuges have a guardian in summer residence who provides a full meals service – details are given within the main text of this guide.

Payment must usually be made in cash as credit cards are not always accepted in mountain huts. Note that banks and/or cash machines can be found in Chamonix, Les Houches, Les Contamines, Courmayeur and La Fouly.

Refuge/hut etiquette
Remove your boots before entering and leave them on a rack in the porch, where you will find a pair of special hut-shoes/slippers to wear. Locate the guardian to book bed-space for the night, and advise him/her of any meals required. There will

sometimes be a choice of menu, but usually not. Blankets and pillows are provided in the dormitory, but not sheets. You are strongly advised to use a sheet sleeping bag (sleeping bag liner) for reasons of hygiene, and to have a head torch with you, as your dormitory may well be unlit. It is usual to pay for accommodation and meals the night before you leave. Refuge guardians will usually phone ahead to reserve a place at the next hut if required.

As for **camping**, there are several authorised campsites along the route, and once again these are indicated in this guide. Off-site camping is not permitted in the Vallée de l'Arve, the Vallée des Glaciers or in any of the Swiss or Italian valleys visited by the TMB.

LANGUAGES

Despite the fact that the Tour of Mont Blanc involves walking in three different countries, the French language is common to each of the valleys visited. 'Mont Blanc has but one tongue', they say, and that may be your experience, but Italian is naturally the preferred language between Col de la Seigne and the Grand Col Ferret.

Do not expect English to be readily understood by those whom you meet in hotels, gîtes, huts or shops, but if, like me, your linguistic skills are embarrassingly poor, brush up on the basics of French before going.

(A French–English glossary of useful words is provided at the back of this book under Appendix D.) An effort to communicate in the host country's language, no matter how poorly, will be appreciated.

MAPS AND WAYMARKS

The complete route of the TMB is contained on a single sheet at 1:50,000 scale. Published by Rando Éditions in conjunction with IGN (the Institut Géographique National), the number is A1, and has the title *Pays du Mont Blanc*. The route is clearly outlined in red, with huts and campsites also marked and the sheet is GPS compatible. There are also two 1:25,000 IGN maps covering the route.

Another one-sheet coverage of the TMB route is to be found on a 1:60,000 map published by Éditions Libris with IGN cartography, and assistance from the Association Grande Traversée des Alpes: number 02 *Mont Blanc*. Swiss and Italian maps also show the route but the French maps are clearer.

The route has been waymarked with varying degrees of enthusiasm and efficiency, and is either in the form of red–white bands painted on rocks, trees or buildings; or a yellow diamond outlined in black bearing the letters TMB. Sometimes an accompanying arrow indicates the direction of travel.

In the Swiss section metal signposts are used at major trail junctions, and the TMB route will be indicated on the finger post, usually with an indication of the length of time expected to reach the next named location.

As is often the case in mountain regions, waymarks are most prolific where the route is obvious, while on awkward terrain (where signs would be welcome) waymarking is sometimes annoyingly absent. That having been said, route-finding should not cause any undue problems.

Typical Swiss signposting in the Val Ferret (top) and TMB waymark on a boulder

NOTES FOR WALKERS

Although the route circles the highest mountain in Western Europe, no technical mountaineering skills are demanded of the TMB walker. There are, however, several high passes to cross, sections of exposed footpath and, in rare instances, metal ladders, rungs, fixed chains and cables to aid the negotiation of steep and/or challenging passages. The most severe of these is located on the Aiguilles Rouges side of the Chamonix valley between Tré-le-Champ and La Flégère, but a more straightforward alternative stage for anyone nervous about this is offered via Col des Montets.

The most important preparation for tackling the Tour of Mont Blanc concentrates on getting fit, for only if you are physically and mentally tuned for such a route will you gain the maximum enjoyment from it. There are many long, and a number of steep, ascents and descents to contend with, and every stage has its challenge. Taking regular exercise at home will go some way towards conditioning yourself for the route's demands, and the best method of achieving this is by walking – uphill, with a rucksack. By putting some effort into getting fit before starting out on the TMB, you'll find that the way to the first pass can be as enjoyable as the last.

Your choice of equipment will also be important.

- For a start, the type of boot you wear can be a critical factor in your enjoyment of the walk.

Boots need to be comfortable, lightweight, of a good fit and broken in before heading for the Alps. They should provide sound ankle support and have thick cleated soles (Vibram or similar) that have not worn smooth, for as much grip as possible will be required on some sections.

- Good waterproofs form an essential part of any TMB walker's kit, not only as protection against rain or snowfall, but to double as windproofs. Jacket and overtrousers made from a 'breathable' fabric are recommended, but a collapsible umbrella can be extremely useful too – especially for walkers who wear spectacles. In all but the windiest of conditions, an umbrella will keep rain off the upper part of your body, protect the top of the rucksack and ensure your glasses do not steam up. Having regularly used a lightweight, collapsible umbrella in high mountain regions throughout the world over a number of years, I am convinced of its usefulness.

- A warm pullover, fleece or pile jacket should also be taken, as should a woollen hat or balaclava, plus gloves. In the summer, wear light-weight layers that can be removed in hot weather.

- Apart from protection against wet and cold, one should also be prepared for extremes of sunshine and heat. A brimmed sunhat,

Arriving at the top of the Fenêtre d'Arpette from Champex

suncream (Factor 20 or stronger), lipsalve and sunglasses ought to form an essential part of your equipment.

- A first-aid kit must be included. Waterbottle (1 litre minimum capacity), compass, headtorch with spare batteries and bulb, whistle and maps should also be carried, as should a small amount of emergency food and a knife. The food can be recharged on occasion, either at a mountain hut or as you pass through villages. A sheet sleeping bag (sleeping bag liner) is advised for nights spent in mountain huts and dortoirs.

- Telescopic trekking poles are extremely useful, particularly when descending steep slopes, and are recommended. One or two poles – choose to suit your own preference.

- As for the rucksack, this needs to fit comfortably and have a waist-belt adjusted to take the weight and control any unnecessary movement when walking. It need not be a large sack, since it ought to be possible to keep all equipment down to an absolute maximum weight of 10kg (20lbs) – unless you intend to camp, that is. A waterproof stuffsac or large thick polythene bag to contain equipment inside the pack will safeguard items from getting wet in the event of bad weather, and a waterproof rucksack cover will form an outer layer of protection. A selection of plastic bags of assorted sizes will be useful.

29

On the ladders between Le Brévent and Col du Brévent

SAFETY IN THE MOUNTAINS

By far the majority of walkers who set out on the TMB complete their tour without anything untoward happening to them, but it should be acknowledged that all mountain regions have their objective dangers, and no one should take them lightly. The route may be well trodden and have ample waymarks, but it also passes through some wild and uninhabited places where an accident could have serious consequences. The following list of dos and don'ts are merely common-sense suggestions based on years of experience, and are offered as a means of avoiding mishaps. With a little attention to detail, the chances are that you'll have nothing more distressing than a small blister to deal with.

Plan each day's walk with care. Study the route details, giving particular attention to the amount of height to be gained and lost, and the estimated time needed to reach your destination. Don't over-estimate your own physical ability or that of your companions, but make an allowance for delays and interruptions, for bad weather and imperfect trail conditions in order to have sufficient time to reach shelter before nightfall.

Check the weather forecast before setting out. This is often posted in mountain refuges, or, failing that, it should be available from the guardian in charge. In a town or village, the tourist office and mountain guides' bureaux will usually display a two- or three-day forecast.

Don't venture onto exposed ridges if a storm is imminent, but in the unlucky event of being caught out by one, avoid isolated trees, prominent rocks and metal objects (discard trekking poles), and do not shelter in caves, beneath overhanging rocks or in gullies. Instead, kneel or squat on your rucksack, with head down and hands on knees.

Carry a few emergency rations and a first-aid kit. (It would be sensible to invest in good first-aid training – not just for the TMB, but for everyday emergencies.) Know how to read a map and compass, and watch for signs of deteriorating weather along the way. Never be too proud to turn back should it be safer to do so than to continue in the face of an on-coming storm or on a trail that has become unjustifiably dangerous.

Keep to approved paths, avoid taking shortcuts and don't venture onto glaciers. When travelling in a group, stay together and be vigilant to signs of fatigue or ill-health among others with you.

In the unhappy event of an accident, stay calm. Move yourself and the victim (if feasible and with care not to aggravate the injury) away from any imminent danger of stonefall or avalanche, and apply immediate first aid. Keep the victim warm, using whatever spare clothes are available. If you're in a party, make a careful written note of the precise location where the victim can be found, and either phone for assistance or send for help while someone remains with the injured member. Should a mountain hut or farm be nearby, seek assistance there. If valley habitation is nearer, find a telephone and dial:

- 112 for general emergencies
- For mountain rescue, the number in Italy is 118, in Switzerland helicopter rescue (REGA) can be summoned by calling 1414.

Should it be impossible to go for help, the international distress signal (given at the front of this book) is: six blasts on a whistle (and flashes with a torch after dark) spaced evenly for one minute, followed by a minute's pause. Repeat for as long as is necessary.

The response is three signals per minute followed by a minute's pause. **Please note that once you call for assistance you become responsible for all costs incurred – make sure you have adequate insurance cover. Mountain rescue is not a cheap option.**

The Fenêtre path provides constant views onto the Glacier du Trient

The addresses of several special-ist insurance companies whose poli-cies cover mountain walking/trekking will be found in Appendix B. It is advisable to leave a photocopy of the policy at home with a friend or mem-ber of the family, and take the orig-inal with you. Reduced-cost (some-times free) urgent medical treatment is available to EC citizens carrying a European health insurance card (EHIC), not only in France and Italy, but also in Switzerland. However, payment is usually required at the time of treatment, so be adequately insured. The free booklet, *Health Advice for Travellers*, available from Post Offices in the UK, gives details of entitlement.

USING THIS GUIDE

This guidebook contains all the information needed to make a suc-cessful Tour of Mont Blanc. The route is described in both the tradi-tional anti-clockwise and clockwise directions, and includes most of the accepted alternative or *variante* options.

Stages described follow the 'sug-gested itineraries' (see above), which would enable you to complete the tour in 10 or 11 days. In practice individ-ual stages will be determined by your fitness and walking capability, and the availability of accommodation.

Each stage described in the guide is accompanied by a sketch map of the route. These are intended to be

used in conjunction with the rele-vant IGN maps. A route profile is also provided for each stage, showing the facilities available en route (see route profile key at the front of the guide).

At the beginning of each stage summary information – distance, height gain and loss, approximate time needed for the walk, high point, accommodation and transport options – is provided. Please note that while height readings have been taken from the appropriate maps, distances given are estimates only. When attempting to measure a route which makes dozens of zigzags, it's impossible to be precise. In any case, such distances are largely irrelevant, for the important thing to remember when tackling a route such as this is the number of hours of enjoyment you gain each day is more important than the actual distance covered.

Since most trekkers measure their progress by time, it should be remembered that times quoted here (in the information boxes, on the pro-files and as cumulative totals through the route descriptions) are **approx-imations only** and make no allow-ances for rest stops, photographic interruptions or consultations with the guidebook or map. For these you will need to add another 25–50 per cent to the day's total. Inevitably these times will be seen as slow by some walkers, fast by others, but by comparing your times with those quoted you will soon discover how much our pace differs, and make the necessary adjustments when calculating your own progress along each stage.

Throughout the text route directions 'left' and 'right' refer to the direction of travel, whether in ascent, descent or traverse. However, when used in reference to the banks of rivers or glaciers, 'left' and 'right' indicate the direction of flow (ie. looking downwards). Where doubts might occur a compass direction is also given.

Where a bracketed number is given within the stage-by-stage route directions (for example (1)), this refers to a specific feature or item of interest which is described in more detail in the section 'Places and Items of Interest on the TMB'.

Abbreviations are used sparingly in this guide, but some have necessarily been adopted. While most should be easily understood, the following list is given for clarification:

ATM	Cash machine (Automated Teller Machine)
BMC	British Mountaineering Council
CAF	Club Alpin Français
CAI	Club Alpino Italiano
CAS	Club Alpin Suisse
GR	Grande Randonnées
IGN	Institut Géographique National
PTT	Post Office (Post, Telephone & Telegraph)
TGV	Trains á Grande Vitesse (the French fast train)
TMB	Tour of Mont Blanc

Having made every effort to check the route as described for accuracy, I trust that this guidebook goes to press with all details correct. However, changes are inevitable during the period when it is likely to be in print, with sections of path perhaps re-routed or certain landmarks altered. Any corrections to keep the guide up-to-date will be made in future printings where possible. Should you discover such changes that are necessary, or can recommend additions with regard to accommodation, places of refreshment, and so on, I would very much appreciate a brief note to that effect. A postcard or email sent to me via the publisher (see 'Updates to this Guide' box at the front of this guide) would be gratefully received and acknowledged if you include your address.

INFORMATION AT A GLANCE

Currencies France and Italy use the Euro. In Switzerland it is the Franc (100 Centimes = 1 Sfr). Take plenty of cash for use in mountain huts (as credit cards are not generally accepted) and for incidental shopping. Major credit cards are usually acceptable in hotels, etc. Bear in mind that banks and other exchange facilities are not always accessible throughout the TMB, and where they do exist, they may not be open when needed. Banks and/or cash machines (ATM) will be found in Chamonix, Les Houches, Les Contamines, Courmayeur and La Fouly.

Formalities Passports should be carried for identification purposes, although these are rarely asked for except when changing travellers' cheques or checking in at some hotels. Visas are not needed by UK citizens.

Health precautions No essential innoculations are required. Avoid exposure to too much sun. Top up drinking water from approved sources, or treat before drinking. Carry the European health insurance card to claim emergency medical treatment through local health services in France, Italy and Switzerland. Medical insurance cover is essential, even where reciprocal health agreements exist.

International dialling codes When dialling from the UK: France 0033; Italy 0039; Switzerland 0041. When dialling from France, Italy or Switzerland: UK 0044; US 001; Ireland 00 353.

Languages French is generally spoken along the route of the TMB irrespective of national boundaries, but Italian is more often used on the south side of Mont Blanc.

Mountain huts Book accommodation in advance, and remember to take a sheet sleeping bag.

TMB on the web www.autourdumontblanc.com/en provides useful information on almost every aspect of the TMB.

THE TOUR OF MONT BLANC
ANTI-CLOCKWISE

*The sharply pointed Aiguille Noire de Peuterey
stands spear-like above Lac Combal*

STAGE 1
*Les Houches – Bionnassay –
Les Contamines*

Start point	Les Houches (1007m)
Distance	16km
Height gain	646m
Height loss	633m
Time	5–5½hrs
High point	Col de Voza (1653m)
Accommodation	Les Houches – hotels, dortoirs, gîte, camping
	Chalet-Refuge du Fioux (2hrs 40mins) – gîte
	Col de Voza (2¼–2½hrs) – hotel
	Bionnassay (3hrs) – gîte
	Le Champel (3½hrs) – gîte
	Les Contamines – hotels, dortoirs, gîte, CAF refuge, camping
Transport options	Cableway (Les Houches – Bellevue)
	Train (St-Gervais – Col de Voza)
	Bus (Tresse – Les Contamines)
Alternative route	Col de Voza – Les Contamines via Col de Tricot and Refuge de Miage (see Alternative Stage 1)

Of the two possible routes to Les Contamines-Montjoie, this is the shorter and easier. It's also recommended as the bad-weather alternative, for apart from the crossing of Col de Voza it remains fairly low and has no really exposed country to pass through. It also involves more road-walking than any other stage; but that being said, there are some fine views (weather permitting), attractive hamlets and plenty of accommodation options even before you reach Les Contamines.

Although it does not have the dramatic appeal of the alternative route, this stage is fairly straightforward but demanding enough for a first day, during which newcomers to the Alps will be able to get into their stride and, from a variety of points along the way, gain an impression of the scenic delights that promise much for the days ahead. Just before reaching Col de

Voza, for example, a row of aiguilles that guard Mont Blanc offer themselves for inspection. The Dôme du Goûter and Aiguille de Bionnassay then dominate views on the south side of the col, with the impressive Bionnassay glacier spilling between them, while from the hamlet of Le Champel the whole Val Montjoie is seen ahead, with a hint of the Col du Bonhomme at its southern end.

LES HOUCHES (1) (1007m) Office de tourisme (Tel 04 50 55 50 62; info@leshouches.com; **www.leshouches. com**), hotels, gîte, camping; shops, restaurants, banks, ATM, PTT, railway, buses, téléphèrique. Lower-priced accommodation: Chalet-Refuge Michel Fagot in centre of village, 36 dortoir places, open mid-Dec to end of Sept (Tel 04 50 54 42 28; reservation@gite-fagot.com); Gîte-Auberge le Crêt, 10 dortoir places, 7 beds, open June to end of Sept – see route details below for access (Tel 04 50 55 52 27; aubergelecret@wanadoo.fr); Hotel Les Campanules, 120 beds, open end Dec to mid-Sept (Tel 04 50 54 40 71; hotel-campanules@wanadoo.fr). For a full list of hotels, contact the tourist office.

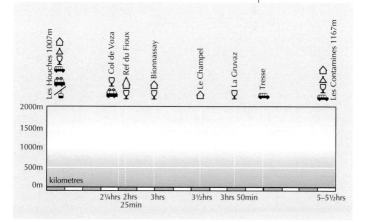

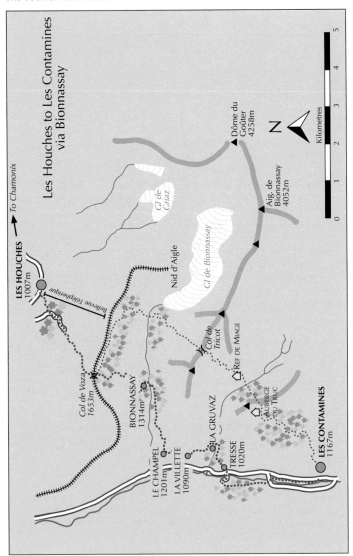

Les Houches to Les Contamines
via Bionnassay

From the railway station cross the road bridge over the river l'Arve and walk uphill into Les Houches, where the tourist office is found in the heart of the village. To reach the start of the TMB continue past the tourist office heading west until you reach the valley station of the Bellevue téléphèrique on the left of the road.

Walk under the road tunnel and continue up the road until you reach 'Le Grand Balcon' where a sign directs you left up steep wooden steps, then along a track. Shortly afterwards turn left up a path, then left again up a road passing some chalets.

The route is now straightforward all the way to the col. As a metalled road it winds up to the chalets of Maison-Neuve, then you fork right on a track that soon enters forest and eventually makes a hairpin at the two buildings of La Tuile (1370m), where a sign gives 55mins to the col. Refreshments are available here at the rustic Restaurant Les Vieilles Luges. The track then continues, fairly steeply in places, all the way to **Col de Voza** (1653m, 2¼–2½hrs, *refreshments, water supply, wc*) with its splendid view back down into the Vallée de l'Arve flanked by a row of aiguilles. A large hotel, the Village de Vacances APAS, dominates the col, while a small bar-restaurant stands beside the line of the Tramway du Mont Blanc **(2)**.

Note If you turn right just before the col you will find, about 30mins to the northwest, the

HOTEL LE PRARION (1860m) 15 dortoir places and 19 beds; open mid-June to early Sept (Tel 04 50 47 40 07; yves@prarion.com). A fine viewpoint.

From the col, cross the tramway line and walk ahead on a dirt road that slopes downhill between woods and open meadows from which you gain impressive views of the Dôme du Goûter, Aiguille de Bionnassay and its glacier **(3)**. About 10mins from the col come to the well-situated

Le Crozat huddles in the shadow of the Aiguille and Glacier de Bionnassay

CHALET-REFUGE DU FIOUX (1520m) accommodation, refreshments: 24 beds; open end of May to end Sept (Tel 04 50 93 52 43).

Continue down to a car park where the track becomes a metalled road. Shortly after this the buildings of Le Crozat are seen to the left, with more fine views – local goat cheese is sometimes for sale here. A few minutes later pass a buvette (La Barmette) and a café, both on the left of the road. These are the first buildings of **Bionnassay** (1314m, 3hrs, *accommodation, refreshments*), a small hamlet nestling just above the narrows of the Bionnassay valley. As the road curves sharply to the right the TMB breaks away left on the Chemin des Tetras. A few paces beyond this turning stands the gîte d'étape

AUBERGE DE BIONNASSAY 27 dortoir places, 18 beds; open June to end Sept (Tel 04 50 93 45 23).

Passing a tiny chapel descend into forest to cross a bridge over the thunderous Bionnassay torrent, then steeply up to a level track/dirt road where you turn right. When you eventually emerge from the forest there's a view down-valley to St-Gervais-les-Bains. Remaining high above the valley you come to **Le Champel** (1201m, 3½hrs, *accommodation*), a neat hamlet of old houses and another tiny chapel with an altar made of logs. A short distance beyond the chapel, where the TMB swings left on the now metalled road, note the

> **GÎTE DU CHAMPEL** 8 dortoir places, 34 beds; open June to mid-Sept (Tel 04 50 47 77 55; gite@champel. fr). See also **LE PECLET**, another gîte with 6 places in 2 rooms; open June to end September (Tel 06 84 18 45 55; lepeclet@orange.fr).

Wandering down the road you gain a fine view ahead along the Val Montjoie **(4)**, but at the first hairpin, leave the road and keep ahead on a track (Chemin des Chevreuils) which leads to **La Villette** (1090m). Veer left in the village by a large water trough and follow the narrow road past chalets, farms and meadows to a minor crossroads on the edge of **La Gruvaz** (3hrs 50mins). Turn left up a narrow track which shortcuts the road bends, and rejoin the road by some houses and another water supply. Bear left as far as a car park, where the road ends at the entrance to the Gorges de la Gruvaz. Cross the bridge spanning a torrent pouring from the unseen Glacier du Miage, and turn immediately right to descend a narrow, damp footpath through forest.

Leave the forest by the first houses of **Tresse** and continue down to the D902, the main road running from St-Gervais to Les Contamines (bus stop nearby). Cross directly ahead and take the Chemin du Quy across the Bon Nant river, then wind uphill to the few houses of **Le Quy**. Here a minor track leaves the road to go straight ahead past a couple of chalets before becoming a footpath. Alternating between forest and pasture the way brings you to the few farms and houses of **Les Hoches**. ▶ Keep ahead on a metalled road between meadows, and about 4½hrs from Les Houches come to a T-junction.

Bear left, and shortly after come to another road at a hairpin by a timber yard. Here you cross the Bon Nant river again by the Pont du Plan de Moulin, and

Alexis Bouvard, the astronomer who discovered the planet Neptune, was born in Les Hoches. (A sign on a building on the left gives details.)

immediately turn right on a riverside path. This is the Sentier de Val Montjoie, which remains among trees and makes a very pleasant approach to Les Contamines. A little under 20mins along this path it forks. If you plan to find accommodation at the CAF's refuge, continue ahead for 15mins, otherwise take the left branch which angles up the slope and brings you into the heart of **Les Contamines-Montjoie (5)** a few paces from the tourist office.

LES CONTAMINES-MONTJOIE (1167m, 5–5½hrs) Office de tourisme (Tel 04 50 47 01 58; info@lescontamines.com; **www.lescontamines.com**) hotels, pensions, dortoirs, gîte, CAF refuge, camping; restaurants, shops (last supplies until Courmayeur), bank, ATM, PTT, bus link with St-Gervais-les-Bains. Lower-priced accommodation: Refuge de la CAF, 28 dortoir places, open mid-June to mid-Sept (Tel 04 50 47 00 88); Chalet Bonaventure, 8 dortoir places, open mid-June to mid-Sept (Tel 04 50 47 23 53; camille.bonaventure@wanadoo.fr). Hotel Christiana, beds and dortoir (Tel 04 50 47 02 72). The Gîte Du Pontet is located at Camping Le Pontet (Tel 04 50 47 04 04; campingdupontet@wanadoo.fr), 2km south of the village: 32 dortoir places, open Jan to late Sept. See Stage 2 for access. For complete hotel details contact the tourist office.

The village of Les Contamines

ALTERNATIVE STAGE 1

Les Houches – Refuge de Miage – Les Contamines

Start point	Les Houches (1007m)
Distance	18km
Height gain	1478m
Height loss	1318m
Time	7½hrs
High point	Col de Tricot (2120m)
Transport options	Cableway (Les Houches – Bellevue)
	Cableway (Les Houches/Les Chavants – Prarion)
	Train (St-Gervais – Col de Voza–Bellevue)
Accommodation	Les Houches – hotels, dortoirs, gîte, camping
	Col de Voza (2¼–2½hrs) – hotel
	Chalets de Miage (5–5½hrs) – refuge
	Truc (6hrs) – auberge
	Les Contamines – hotels, dortoirs, gîte, CAF refuge, camping
Alternative route	Col de Voza – Les Contamines via Bionnassay (see Stage 1)

The bare statistics of height gain and loss, and the amount of time calculated to walk this stage, underline the fact that it's a demanding route for a first day. But it's also a magnificent section, rich in high mountain views and a worthy introduction to the Tour of Mont Blanc. As far as Col de Voza, the route is the same as that for the main TMB, but thereafter the two options are very different. This is a true high route, for the trail ventures close to the world of glacier, moraine and rock, crosses a 2000m pass (Col de Tricot) and avoids permanent habitation until Les Contamines is reached.

One need not go all the way to Les Contamines on this stage and there's much to be said for choosing either Refuge de Miage or Auberge du Truc in which to spend the night, both giving a sense of remote tranquility under the Dômes de Miage.

A note of warning before setting out: check the weather forecast in Les Houches, and if a storm is predicted, opt for the main TMB route via Bionnassay, for there's no real shelter between Col de Voza and the Chalets de Miage, and crossing Col de Tricot in stormy conditions is inadvisable. But if the weather looks good, go for it! It's a great walk.

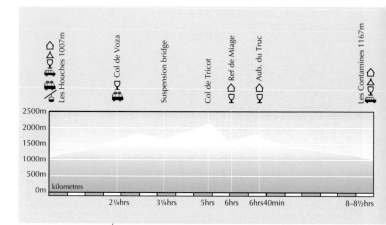

For the route from Les Houches **(1)** to **Col de Voza** (1653m, *refreshments, water supply, wc*), follow directions given under Stage 1 above. Col de Voza is reached in 2¼–2½hrs.

Cross the railway and turn left immediately past the bar-restaurant where a track rises alongside the line of the Tramway du Mont Blanc **(2)**, and about 20mins later come to the refurbished Hotel Bellevue (1786m, *accommodation, refreshments*). The building is well named, for the view all along this ridge is very fine indeed. To the left the Chamonix valley stretches towards Col de Balme, Le Brévent and the Aiguilles Rouges forming the left-hand wall of the valley, the Chamonix Aiguilles on the right, while directly ahead the Dôme du Goûter stands a little left of the rounded snow hump of Mont Blanc itself. Make the most of this view, for it will soon be lost, and you'll not see the Chamonix valley again until you cross the Col de Balme in about eight days' time.

Just beyond the building veer slightly right across a meadow where a path takes you onto a steep, partly wooded hillside that sweeps down into the Bionnassay valley. Making an undulating traverse of the slope, go through a gate and join a second path coming from

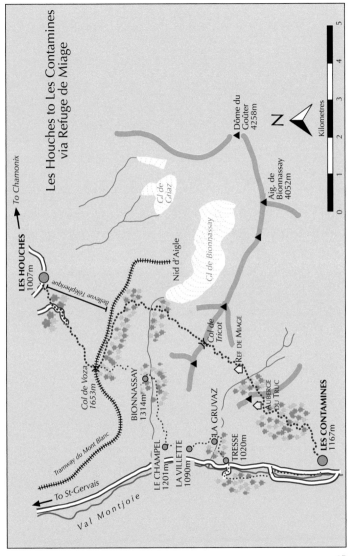

Les Houches to Les Contamines
via Refuge de Miage

This is just the latest in a whole series of bridges across the Bionnassay torrent, the previous incarnations having been destroyed by avalanche or swept away by a spring flood.

Bionnassay. Keep ahead, through another gate and along an easy contour to a T-junction of paths (25mins from Bellevue), where you turn right across an open meadow with splendid views up to the cascading Glacier de Bionnassay **(3)**.

The way now goes onto the wooded lateral moraine bulldozed by the glacier, and descends among trees to a Himalayan-style suspension bridge (1650m) that spans the roaring glacial torrent – a wash of coffee-coloured water spewing from the rubble-strewn snout of the glacier. ◄

Across the bridge the way twists uphill through dense vegetation to another path junction. The right-hand option descends to Bionnassay and Le Champel, but we climb on among trees, now making for Col de Tricot which lies some 400m higher up the hillside. It's a steep climb, but out of the trees the path snakes up grass slopes of the Combe de Tricot dotted with alpenroses, with views of the Aiguilles du Goûter and Bionnassay guarding the upper glacier, while across the valley the line of the Tramway du Mont Blanc is clearly visible.

Col de Tricot (2120m) is reached in about 4-4½hrs from Les Houches. This is a broad, grassy saddle on a long ridge spur stretching down from the Aiguille de Bionnassay, forming a partition between the valleys of Bionnassay to the north and Miage to the south. On the saddle there's a low stone wall and the remains of a one-time building, and from it you look steeply down to the Chalets de Miage huddled almost 600m below on the edge of the Miage pastures.

Numerous zigzags take you down on the south side of the ridge. The gradient is very steep in places and caution is advised, for it's on descents like this, tackled in the early stages of a long trek, that knees can be damaged – especially if you're carrying a reasonably heavy rucksack, as you would if backpacking. Trekking poles, suitably lengthened for such a descent, will help take some of the pressure off.

In the midst of the cluster of buildings that go under the name of the Chalets de Miage you'll find the

REFUGE DE MIAGE (1550m, 5–5½hrs) accommodation, refreshments; 37 dortoir places, 2 rooms; open June to mid-Sept (Tel 04 50 93 22 91).

The refuge has a very fine outlook to the head of the little hanging valley which is topped by the snow-crested Dômes de Miage. The situation is idyllic, and a night spent here is worth considering. Camping may be permitted – enquire at the refuge. From here the TMB path crosses a stream and brings you onto a track where, across a bridge, a signpost directs you left to Le Truc and Les Contamines. This path tacks easily up the walling hillside to the Mont Truc ridge crest, a climb of around 160m, taking about 40mins to reach the

AUBERGE DU TRUC (1720m, 6hrs) accommodation, refreshments; 28 dortoir places; open mid-June to mid-Sept (Tel 04 50 93 12 48).

The Dômes de Miage close the head of the secluded Miage valley

47

The view from Mont Truc ('truc' means rounded summit) at the end of the ridge spur is said to be excellent.

The auberge stands in an open meadow with the Dômes de Miage and their glaciers appearing even closer than they did from the Miage meadows. In the opposite direction the view extends down the Val Montjoie (4) to the lower valley of the Arve. ◄

Walk down the track for about 15mins, and on rounding the first sharp right-hand bend take a path on the left signed to Contamines. This descends a forested hillside and rejoins the track at 1512m. Turn left and wander down the track, or unsurfaced road, for the rest of the descent to a car park at **La Frasse** (1263m, 7hrs), where there's a public toilet and a water supply on the left. Continue down towards Les Contamines, following waymarks past old farm buildings on a stony path that shortcuts the road, then down among houses of the upper part of the village where a series of paths (the Chemin du P'tou) lead all the way to the church in **Les Contamines-Montjoie** (5) a short walk from the tourist office – turn right along the main road for this.

LES CONTAMINES-MONTJOIE (1167m, 7½hrs) Office de tourisme (Tel 04 50 47 01 58; info@ lescontamines.com); hotels, pensions, dortoirs, gîte, CAF refuge, camping; restaurants, shops (last supplies until Courmayeur), bank, ATM, PTT, bus link with St-Gervais-les-Bains. Lower-priced accommodation: Refuge du CAF, 28 dortoir places, open mid-June to mid-Sept (Tel 04 50 47 00 88); Chalet Bonaventure, 8 dortoir places, open mid-June to mid-Sept (Tel 04 50 47 23 53; camille.bonaventure@wanadoo. fr). Hotel Christiania, beds (Tel 04 50 47 02 72, hotel-christiania@wanadoo.fr; www. lechristiania-hotel.com). The Gîte Du Pontet is located at Camping Le Pontet (Tel 04 50 47 04 04; campingdupontet@wanadoo.fr), 2km south of the village: 32 dortoir places, open June to late Sept. See Stage 2 for access details. For complete hotel details contact the tourist office, which also produces an annual accommodation list for the whole TMB.

STAGE 2

Les Contamines – Col de la Croix du Bonhomme – Les Chapieux

Start point	Les Contamines (1167m)
Distance	18km or 20km via Col des Fours to Refuge des Mottets
Height gain	1316m (or 1579m)
Height loss	929m (or 876m)
Time	7–7½hrs or 7½–8hrs via Col des Fours *variante*
High point	Col de la Croix du Bonhomme 2483m or Col des Fours 2665m
Transport option	Bus (Les Contamines – Notre-Dame de la Gorge)
Accommodation	Pontet (40mins) – gîte d'étape, camping
	Nant-Borrant (1½hrs) – chalet/gîte
	La Balme (2½hrs) – chalet/gîte
	Col de la Croix (5–5½hrs) – CAF refuge
	Les Chapieux – auberge /refuge, camping
	Les Mottets (7½–8hrs) – refuge (Col des Fours option)
Alternative route	Col de la Croix du Bonhomme – Col des Fours – Refuge des Mottets (see below)

On this stage the TMB goes right to the head of Val Montjoie and crosses over into the Vallée des Glaciers by way of Col du Bonhomme and Col de la Croix du Bonhomme. Although more challenging than Stage 1 (via Bionnassay), it does not equal the high-route alternative first stage in physical demands, but it's a reasonably tough crossing nonetheless. Early in the season snow will no doubt remain in patches between the two cols, in which case special care will need to be taken. Just below the highest of these the Refuge de la Croix du Bonhomme commands a splendid position and makes a good alternative overnight option, although Les Chapieux has a relaxing atmosphere on a bend in the Vallée des Glaciers, but without any noteworthy views.

On arrival at Col de la Croix du Bonhomme, a TMB *variante* ignores the descent to Les Chapieux and rises to the barren Col des Fours before descending to the valley at Ville des Glaciers, an hour or so upvalley beyond Les Chapieux. Walkers taking this option will probably choose to continue to Refuge des Mottets for accommodation. Under good snow-free conditions the Col des Fours route makes a worthy alternative to the standard crossing, but early in the season, or in inclement weather or poor visibility, the main route to Les Chapieux should be taken. Both options are described.

South of Les Contamines cross the river on a footbridge by the first road bridge after leaving the main village, then follow the river upstream for about 10mins. For accommodation at the comfortable Chalet-Hotel La Chemenaz (Tel 04 50 47 02 44), turn right; the hotel is about 2mins' walk away. Cross to the left side and resume on a tree-lined path which soon swings left to bring you parallel with the road. When the road makes a sharp right-hand turn to cross the river by a carpark at the entrance to the Parc de Loisirs du Pontet, walk ahead on a good broad and level path, soon passing a water supply. A little later note a small lake on the right, with a bar/restaurant on its shore. Camping Le Pontet and its gîte (see details at the end of the previous stage) are not far from here. About 45mins from Les Contamines reach a junction of paths

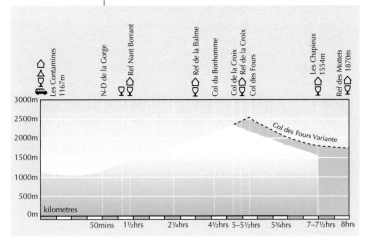

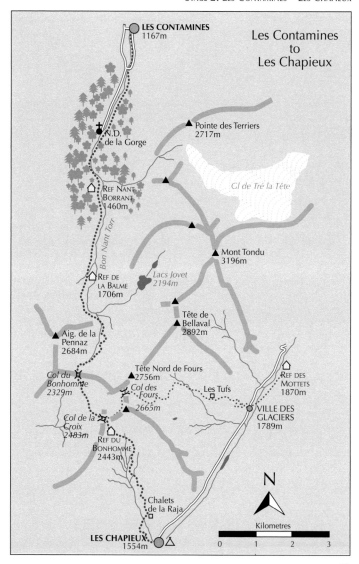

Les Contamines
to
Les Chapieux

LES CONTAMINES
1167m

● N.D.
de la Gorge

▲ Pointe des Terriers
2717m

Gl de Tré la Tête

⌂ REF NANT
BORRANT
1460m

▲

Bon Nant Torr

▲

▲ Mont Tondu
3196m

⌂ REF DE
LA BALME
1706m

*Lacs Jovet
2194m*

▲

▲ Tête de
Bellaval
2892m

▲ Aig. de la
Pennaz
2684m

▲ Tête Nord de Fours
2756m

⌂ REF DES
MOTTETS
1870m

*Col du
Bonhomme
2329m*

*Col des
Fours*

□ Les Tufs

● VILLE DES
GLACIERS
1789m

▲
2665m

*Col de la
Croix
2483m*

⌂ REF DU
BONHOMME
2443m

N

□ Chalets
de la Raja

LES CHAPIEUX
1554m ▲

Kilometres

0   1   2   3

51

This tree-fringed lake lies beside the route between Les Contamines and Notre-Dame de la Gorge

near the pilgrimage chapel of **Notre-Dame de la Gorge (6)** (1210m). Should you need refreshment, there's a café-restaurant next to the chapel.

The TMB path now rises directly ahead up the steep left-hand side of a wooded ravine on Roman-laid slabs, passing a rock arch (Pont Naturel) to the right, then easing to cross the hump-backed Pont de la Téna about 10mins before coming to the Alpinus Lodge (*refreshments*) and, shortly after, an attractive chalet-style building in a neat garden on the right:

REFUGE NANT BORRANT (1460m, 1½hrs) accommodation, refreshments; 35 dortoir places; open early June to late Sept (Tel 04 50 47 03 57; refugenantborrant@free.fr).

At this point you enter the Réserve Naturelle des Contamines-Montjoie **(7)**. Here you cross a stream, rise a little further and, 10mins from Nant Borrant the way forks. A sign here indicates that overnight camping is permitted 100m down to the left; a very pleasant site just above the river. The TMB continues along the right branch, easing into a stretch of open meadowland with the shapely Aiguilles de la Pennaz ahead. Near the far end of this level stretch there's a water supply on the left of the track. About 20mins beyond this, having climbed again, a sign indicates another *emplacement de bivouac* (overnight campsite) 100m to the right. By the main track note another water supply and a small public toilet block, just above which you will come to the

REFUGE DE LA BALME (1706m, 2¼hrs) accommodation, refreshments; 36 dortoir places, 14 beds; open mid-June to mid-Sept (Tel 04 50 47 03 54).

The jeep track loops up the hillside, but about 2mins beyond La Balme a footpath breaks away on the left and ascends steeply over rough ground with stony zigzags for 30mins or so until reaching a bluff with an electricity pylon. About 5mins beyond the pylon the way forks. Both routes merge a little higher across a basin running

In the upper Val Montjoie the Aiguille de la Pennaz dominates

The route between Col du Bonhomme and the higher Col de la Croix du Bonhomme

with streams – the right-hand path, which crosses a stream or two, can be rather marshy at times, but it also leads through a veritable flower garden in the early summer. This basin is known as the Plan Jovet, and off to the left a cascade can be seen pouring from a hanging valley that contains the two Lacs Jovet – a picturesque spot. Ignoring this, the TMB climbs through a narrow rocky section to the Plan des Dames, marked by a huge pile of stones said to be on the spot where an English woman perished in a storm. Tossing a stone onto the pile is something of a ritual – as it is in mountain country throughout the world.

Col du Bonhomme is clearly visible almost 300m above, and large patches of snow often lie across the slopes leading to it. Across the Plan des Dames the path takes the right-hand side of the valley, and, as height is gained, so the way breaks into several strands rising across shaly slopes to converge on the saddle of **Col du Bonhomme** (2329m, 4½hrs), where there's a small wooden shelter. In good conditions this is a charming place; a broad saddle between the Rocher du Bonhomme and Bancs de la Pennaz, with long views down through the Val Montjoie to the north, and Vallon de la Gittaz in the Beaufortain district to the southwest. A path drops into this latter valley, brightened by the Lac de la Gittaz and much more extensive Lac de Roselend, while our path still has more height to gain.

Bear left along the saddle and begin rising once more into a wilder, more stony region of scree and rocks and, quite possibly, a few late-lying snow patches. In misty conditions this can seem an eerie place, but on a good day the route is one to enjoy, with anticipation of the next pass luring you on as views grow in extent. Minor streams drain across the path, and about 45mins from Col du Bonhomme you come to the large cairn which marks the summit of **Col de la Croix du Bonhomme** (2483m, 5–5¼hrs). Before you the hillside folds down to the hinted Vallée des Glaciers, while mountains, ridges and other valleys of Beaufortain provide a very different landscape to that which you've left behind. To the south Mont Pourri dominates.

Refuge de la Croix du Bonhomme lies just 50m and 5mins below on the south side of the ridge, but before descending to it, a decision must be made as to the continuing route, options being:
- via Col des Fours to Refuge des Mottets (see box), or
- the standard TMB route to Les Chapieux via Refuge de la Croix (see main route description below).

The first option is a little longer than the standard route, but as it reduces Stage 3 by about 1½hrs, and avoids a stretch of road-walking, it might be preferred. However, Col des Fours should not be attempted if much snow is lying, nor if there's any threat of bad weather or poor visibility. The second option is a fine route in any case, but one also has the possibility of spending the night at Refuge de la Croix du Bonhomme, and making a decision as to the continuing route next day.

Main route to Les Chapieux
From Col de la Croix du Bonhomme it is only a 5min walk down to the refuge. Unless snow has obscured it the path,

TMB VARIANTE: COL DES FOURS – REFUGE DES MOTTETS

Bear left at Col de la Croix and go up the ridge crest to an electricity pylon. Beyond this the way cuts along the left (west) flank of Tête Sud des Fours to gain the bare saddle of **Col des Fours** (2665m, 5¾hrs), about 35mins from Col de la Croix. Along with the Fenêtre d'Arpette (Alt. Stage 8), this is the highest point reached on the TMB, and from it Mont Blanc can be seen to the northeast beyond the Aiguille des Glaciers, a shining dome of snow and ice. Should you have sufficient time and energy, it's worth continuing as far as the 2756m summit of Tête Nord des Fours **(8)**, where the 360° panorama is magnificent. (Allow 40mins for the round trip from Col des Fours.)

Cross the col and descend southeastwards on steep slopes of shale and, possibly, snow patches towards the basin of Plan des Fours. After losing about 250m of height, veer left when the path forks, cross a stream that drops through a gully, and then descend steeply alongside, then across, the Tufs stream and over pastures to the deserted alp buildings of **Les Tufs** (1993m), about 1–1¼hrs from Col des Fours. Here you join a farm road and wander down it to more farm buildings that go by the grand name of **La Ville des Glaciers** (1789m, 7½hrs). (Note the public toilets in the small car park.) Cross the road and go down to the Torrent des Glaciers on a track which crosses the river and rises gently to the atmospheric converted dairy farm of **Refuge des Mottets** (1870m, 8hrs, accommodation, refreshments; 90 places; open mid-June to mid-Sept; (04 79 07 01 70; refuge@lesmottets.com).

which descends southward, is easy to follow and soon brings you to

REFUGE DE LA CROIX DU BONHOMME (9)
(2443m, 5–5¼hrs) accommodation, refreshments; 113 dortoir places; manned mid-June to mid-Sept; (Tel 04 79 07 05 28; refuge-bonhomme@free.fr).

A rather curious-looking building, it enjoys a commanding position, and the view from it, whilst not containing any dramatic mountains, is charming – especially in the soft light of evening.

The path veers left at the refuge to negotiate a series of grassy bluffs and streams before descending fairly steeply to the south on the way to the Chalets de Plan

Varraro (alp buildings) at 2006m. Passing these to your left the path drops steeply once more to another group of buildings, the **Chalets de la Raja** (1789m, 6½hrs), where you bear right, cross a bridge and come onto a stony jeep track. Follow this round the hillside to the left until coming to a junction where you take the lower option (sign to Refuge La Nova). Keep alert for a footpath that drops through pastures on the left, and brings you to the hamlet of **Les Chapieux** on a bend in the Vallée des Glaciers **(10)**, directly opposite the Auberge de la Nova.

LES CHAPIEUX (1554m, 7–7½hrs) accommodation, refreshments in Auberge de la Nova, 35 dortoir places, 35 beds; open May to early Oct; (Tel 04 79 89 07 15; info@refugelanova.com); Chambres du Soleil, 14 beds (Tel 04 79 31 22; lesoleildeschapieux@gmail.com); camping permitted in meadows below the hamlet – public toilet block next to a seasonal tourist office; small grocery.

NO LONGER A 'WRETCHED LITTLE HAMLET'

When AW Moore and his guide, Christian Almer, came to Les Chapieux in July 1864 on their way from Bourg St Maurice to the Pavillon Bellevue above Col de Voza (an epic walk of 10½hrs), Moore was unimpressed, calling it a 'wretched little hamlet'. It was 8.40 in the morning, and the two men, in need of refreshment, went into the 'larger of the two little inns [which] has a bad reputation, and, according to our experience, deservedly so. I ordered an omelette and a bottle of red wine,' said Moore, 'and in lieu of the latter was furnished with a chopine of what was perfect vinegar, of the sourest and most undrinkable character, which not even a copious mixture of water could make palatable, much less wholesome. The charge was extortionate, and at 9.15 we departed, congratulating ourselves that we were not compelled to make a long halt in such a den of thieves, the situation of which is most dreary and devoid of interest.' (*The Alps* in 1864)

Happily, the experience of TMB walkers in Les Chapieux today is unlikely to mirror that of the unfortunate AW Moore.

STAGE 3
Les Chapieux – Col de la Seigne – Rifugio Elisabetta

Start point	Les Chapieux (1554m)
Distance	15km
Height gain	1004m
Height loss	258m
Time	4½–5hrs
High point	Col de la Seigne (2516m)
Accommodation	Les Mottets (2hrs) – privately-owned refuge
	Rifugio Elisabetta – CAI refuge

On this stage the TMB crosses out of France and enters Italy at the Col de la Seigne, one of the easiest crossings of the circuit, but one which also happens to be among the most scenic. Given reasonable visibility, the view of Mont Blanc and the Aiguille Noire from Col de la Seigne is stunning, and is seen at its best early in the morning.

This relatively short stage will enable you to relax a little after what will have been two fairly demanding days, and there's a good chance you'll arrive at Rifugio Elisabetta with plenty of time in hand.

Walk out of Les Chapieux heading northeast along the road, shortly joining company with the river and entering a defile which is, in effect, the demarcation between the lower and upper valleys. Less than 1km from Les Chapieux take a signed footpath on the right which entices you off the road, exchanging what would otherwise be a slog on tarmac, for a more pleasant walk. The path climbs some way above the road before sloping down to cross the river on a fine bridge, then continues heading upstream through the Vallée des Glaciers, at the head of which the pinnacle of the Aiguille des Glaciers is the most prominent feature. Soon the Col de la Seigne appears to the right of the aiguille. Drawing level with the few farm buildings of **La Ville des Glaciers** (1789m, 1½hrs), the footpath comes onto a track feeding from the road. It is here that the Col des Fours

variante joins the main route. There's a toilet block just across the bridge here, and an opportunity to top up water bottles. Apart from the refuge 30mins ahead, there will be no further guaranteed supply until you reach Rifugio Elisabetta.

The small hamlet of Les Chapieux nestles on a bend in the Vallée des Glaciers

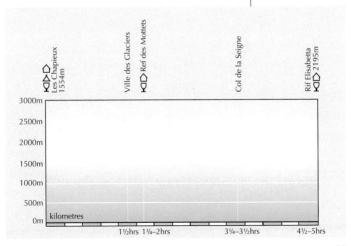

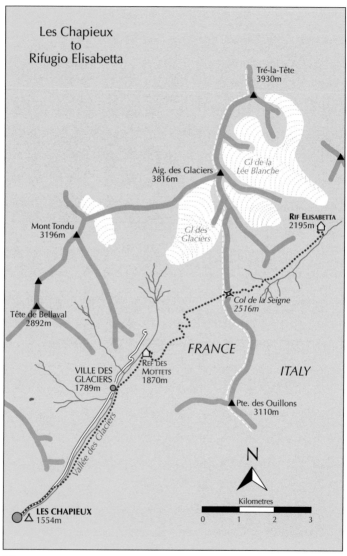

Les Chapieux
to
Rifugio Elisabetta

Tré-la-Tête
3930m

Gl de la
Lée Blanche

Aig. des Glaciers
3816m

RIF ELISABETTA
2195m

Mont Tondu
3196m

Gl des
Glaciers

Col de la Seigne
2516m

Tête de Bellaval
2892m

FRANCE

ITALY

REF DES
MOTTETS
1870m

VILLE DES
GLACIERS
1789m

Pte. des Ouillons
3110m

Vallée des Glaciers

N

Kilometres

0   1   2   3

LES CHAPIEUX
1554m

The valley's upper basin now spreads out to reveal the rocky eminence of Mont Tondu, above to the left; a pastoral area that encroaches as far as the outliers of the Mont Blanc massif. Follow the track ahead to the ruins of a one-time hotel and continue to the former dairy farm that has been converted to the

REFUGE DES MOTTETS (1870m, 2hrs) accommodation, refreshments; 90 dortoir places; open mid-June to mid-Sept (Tel 04 79 07 01 70; www.lesmottets.com).

This is an atmospheric place for a night's lodging, with a dining room decorated with an assortment of old cheese-making implements, and the former cowshed turned into a dormitory. As it is the only place for refreshments between Les Chapieux and Rifugio Elisabetta, it's worth stopping to tank up before heading for the pass.

From here the route to the col is neither long nor particularly arduous, although it has a few short, steep sections. Initially a broad, well-graded path, it later breaks into a skein of often muddy trails. Ascending high pastures, it dips into a stream-cut ravine and eases up the final broad slope that leads to the **Col de la Seigne (11)** (2516m, 3¼–3½hrs) and the revelation of a new world.

Arrival at the col is an eye-opener. Standing on the borders of France and Italy views in all directions are magnificent. Directly ahead the hillside falls away into a long, deep trench that forms a moat to the southern bastions of the Mont Blanc range. Immediately below the col the Vallon de la Lée Blanche, guarded by the Pyramides Calcaires, spills into the Vel Veni, which in itself leads to the (Italian) Val Ferret, at whose head the Grand Col Ferret will be crossed in another three days' time. Beyond that rise Mont Vélan and the Grand Combin. Along the right-hand wall of this 'moat' a rumpled green hillside carries the route of the TMB, while the left-hand wall boasts a succession of astonishingly rugged peaks and spiky ridges interrupted by cascades of ice and grey moraines. Dominant in all this is the graceful iced dome of Mont Blanc itself, with the spectacular

An early morning cloud-sea below Col de la Seigne fills the Val Veni

Aiguille Noire de Peuterey running a close second. The scene is exquisite and dominated by verticals.

Given calm settled weather, Col de la Seigne is not an easy place to leave. In snow-free conditions the path down into the Vallon de la Lée Blanche is easy to follow, but if visibility is poor, or snow patches remain on the east side, care should be taken on the initial descent. There are, in fact, several braidings at first, but these come together lower down as a good path. About 10mins from the col the waymarked path goes alongside a renovated former customs house, La Casermetta (2365m). This is now used as a museum and mountain information centre, and is worth a short visit. The way continues down into the pastures of Lée (or Lex) Blanche, the uppermost reaches of the Val Veni. Other writers have dismissed this valley as either dreary, wild, a desolate combe, or as having a melancholy character. I find it excitingly full of promise. Delineated by streams, the pastures are grazed by cattle in summer, and as you wander across the level grasslands, cowbells ringing in your ears, so your attention is drawn time and again to the great rocky spear of the Aiguille Noir ahead.

The levels of Lée Blanche end at the cluster of old buildings known as the Alpe inférieur de la Lex Blanche (2258m). Turn sharp left here and ascend a narrow path for about 10mins to reach the

RIFUGIO ELISABETTA (2195m, 4½–5hrs) accommodation, refreshments; 53 dortoir places, 20 beds; manned mid-June to mid-Sept (Tel 01 65 84 40 80; info@rifugioelisabetta.com). Owned and staffed by the Milan section of the CAI the rifugio, officially named Elisabetta Soldini, overlooks the lower Vallon de la Lée Blanche from a spur extending from one of the Pyramides Calcaires, and is backed by the Glacier d'Estellette and Glacier de la Lée Blanche. Despite its stated capacity, the number of visitors may well exceed this in the high season. Sunset views can be magical.

Rifugio Elisabetta stands on a spur overlooking the Vallon de la Lée Blanche

STAGE 4
Rifugio Elisabetta – Courmayeur

Start point	Rifugio Elisabetta (2195m)
Distance	18km or 20km via Rifugio Monte Bianco
Height gain	460m
Height loss	1560m
Time	5–5½hrs
High point	Mont Favre spur (2430m)
Transport options	Bus (La Visaille – Courmayeur)
	Cablecar (Plan Chécrouit – Courmayeur)
Accommodation	Lac Combal (45 mins) – gîte/refuge
	Col Chécrouit (3¾hrs) – privately-owned gîte-refuge
	Val Veni (2–2½hrs) – camping, gîte, hotel (Val Veni option)
	Val Veni (4¼hrs) – CAI refuge (Rifugio Monte Bianco option)
	Dolonne (5hrs) – hotel
	Courmayeur – hotels, pensions
Alternative routes	via Val Veni all the way to Courmayeur – a bad-weather 'escape' route (see below).
	Col Chécrouit – Rif. Monte Bianco – Courmayeur (see below)

Although there are no passes to cross on this stage, and the amount of height gain is modest, the undulating nature of the high route along the south flank of the Val Veni can make this seem a fairly demanding day.

This is a wonderfully varied walk among scenery of the highest order. It begins by dropping into the lower Vallon de la Lée Blanche, where a tracery of streams combine to create the so-called Lac Combal, backed by the monstrous wall of moraine thrown up by the Glacier de Miage that spills into the valley between gateways of rock. On gaining the foot of this moraine wall, the TMB then swings to the right and climbs steeply up the right-hand hillside, passes two groups of derelict alp buildings and continues until reaching a high point on a spur coming from Mont Favre. From here to Col Chécrouit the route follows a balcony path of immense appeal – every step further unravels a sumptuous view of 'the disordered and magnificent cluster of the great peaks, and of Mont Blanc itself', as Roger Frison-Roche once described it. Two or three small pools lie along this hillside to create a mirror image of the aiguilles and snowpeaks opposite.

At Col Chécrouit the main route as described descends to Courmayeur via the attractive village of Dolonne, while an alternative option (also described) invites walkers down into Val Veni to skirt the northern base of Mont Chétif, and then to approach Courmayeur from the north.

Finally, should the weather be very bad, you are advised to ignore the 'high route' as described beyond Lac Combal, and remain in the bed of Val Veni throughout – a walk of about 3½–4hrs from Rifugio Elisabetta; outline details given below.

Out of the refuge descend to the buildings of Alpe inférieur, where an unmetalled road, built by the Italian army, comes up from Lac Combal. Footpath shortcuts enable you to avoid most of the road-walking until you reach the valley floor, but thereafter you can swing easily along, either on the road itself or its grassy verge, almost as far as a stone bridge at 1950m at the northern end of the milky-blue Lac Combal below the wall of lateral moraine. This is reached in about 45mins. Despite the

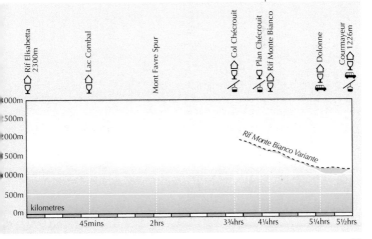

65

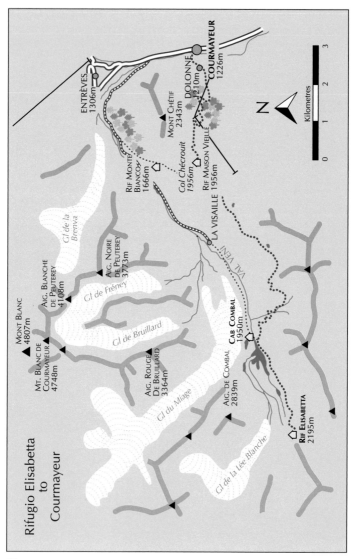

Rifugio Elisabetta to Courmayeur

MONT BLANC 4807m

MT. BLANC DE COURMAYEUR 4748m

AIG. BLANCHE DE PEUTEREY 4108m

AIG. NOIRE DE PEUTEREY 3773m

Gl de la Brenva

Gl de Fréney

Gl de Bruillard

AIG. ROUGE DE BRUILLARD 3364m

Gl du Miage

AIG. DE COMBAL 2839m

Gl de la Lée Blanche

CAB COMBAL 1950m

RIF ELISABETTA 2195m

VAL VÉNY

LA VISAILLE

RIF MONTE BIANCO 1666m

Col Chécrouit 1956m

RIF MAISON VIEILLE 1956m

MONT CHÉTIF 2343m

ENTRÈVES 1306m

DOLONNE 1210m

COURMAYEUR 1226m

N

0 1 2 3

Kilometres

Lac Combal and the Aiguille Noire de Peuterey

road (which can be horribly dusty following a spell of dry weather), the landscape is of such value that your attention is likely to be anywhere but on the road itself. The TMB turns off shortly before the bridge.

On the other side of the river accommodation and refreshments are available at **Caban du Combal** (1950m 45 mins) 23 dorm places, open June to September (Tel 01 65 17 56 421; cabaneducombal@gmail.com).

TMB Bad-Weather Option: Val Veni To Courmayeur

From the bridge at the northern end of Lac Combal, walk down the road for about 30mins, then take a footpath on the right descending briefly through larch-woods to rejoin the road a little lower. About 10mins later enter the hamlet of **La Visaille** from where there's a bus service to Courmayeur. A few paces beyond Chalet del Miage (*refreshments*) a signed footpath descends on the left, leading downvalley in another 30mins or so to **Camping La Sorgente** and its gîte (8 dortoir places, 22 beds, open June to mid-Sept Tel 01 65 86 90 89;

info@campingsorgente.net). Continuing down the road, when it makes a left-hand hairpin just out of La Visaille, note a path/track which goes straight ahead for another 45mins to reach **Rifugio Monte Bianco** (1666m, 14 dortoir places, 50 beds; open mid-June to mid-Sept Tel 01 65 86 90 97). The road snakes downhill with footpath shortcuts, and comes to **Camping Aiguille Noire** (with on-site refreshments and shop; Tel 01 65 869 014; www.aiguillenoire.com), before passing a side road on the left going to **Pertud** (Peuterey; 1502m), Camping Monte Bianco La Sorgente, the gîte mentioned above, and two hotels. About 20mins later you pass below the pilgrimage chapel of Notre Dame de la Guerison, and in another hour reach **Courmayeur** (see main route for details).

Main route to Courmayeur
For the TMB high route take the path which you will see on the right about 50m before the bridge. It angles up the vegetated hillside and in a little under 20mins brings you to the ruins of Alpe inférieur de l'Arp Vieille, then more directly up the slope before crossing a stream, and climbing again to Alpe supérieure de l'Arp Vieille (2303m, 1¾hrs) – another abandoned building with an outlook across the valley directly onto the Miage glacier. The whole southern face of the Mont Blanc range is being revealed now, and the higher you climb the more of it you see and the more one gains a true impression of the vast scale of these mountains. In the Himalaya one would need to walk for many a long day to capture such a vision as you will see from this high path.

Above Alpe supérieure the way rises further to pass above a small pool, then angles leftward up a spur projecting from Mont Favre. Rounding this about 30mins or so above Alpe supérieure, you attain the highest point on the walk at 2430m. From here the full sweeping majesty of crag, spire, snow-dome, rockface and nosing glacier that makes up the north wall of the Vals Veni and Ferret is laid before you. Yet this is just one vantage point among many to be visited on the walk to Courmayeur.

Moving on, the path slopes down into a combe, crosses a stream on stepping stones where the water has cut a groove, then rises over a grass bluff to pass another small pool off to the right (a photographer's delight). Mostly over grass slopes, but sometimes among trees, the path meanders on, passes below Lac Chécrouit, and continues towards Col Chécrouit, which is found at the foot of a minor wooded slope.

Morning light on the Aiguille Noire, seen across the Val Veni from Col Chécrouit

Col Chécrouit (1956m, 3¾hrs, *accommodation, refreshments*) is a wonderful location with a view across the valley into the armchair-like hollow known as the Fauteuil des Allemands on the face of the Aiguille Noire de Peuterey, and south through the narrows of Val d'Aosta to outliers of the Gran Paradiso range. Overnight accommodation may be had in the privately-owned

RIFUGIO MAISON VIEILLE 50 dortoir places; open from mid-June to end Sept (Tel 337 23 09 79; info@maisonvieille.com; **www.maisonvieille.com**).

Nearby the slopes have been laced with cableways, and bulldozed pistes scar the hillsides as a direct contrast to the untamed landscapes walked thus far.

There are two ways to proceed from here:

- descend leftwards to Rifugio Monte Bianco and Notre Dame de la Guérison in the Val Veni, then round the base of Mont Chétif to Courmayeur (see 'TMB *variante*' box below), or
- go ahead and right to Plan Chécrouit on tracks and footpaths, then down to Dolonne and Courmayeur (described in the next section).

The first takes a little longer than the second and has more close views of the big mountains, but at the same time has more roadwork to contend with. The Plan Chécrouit/Dolonne option descends at first through ski terrain, but as a 'plus' visits Dolonne, which is a truly charming village. This route also gives an opportunity (for those who want it) of a cablecar ride down to the valley.

TMB VARIANTE: COURMAYEUR VIA RIFUGIO MONTE BIANCO

Turn sharp left at the Maison Vieille refuge, and walk across the meadows to where a path leads steeply downhill among trees to a ski-lift in a clearing. Go down the bank, then turn right onto a broad slope running down to the CAI-owned

RIFUGIO MONTE BIANCO (1666m, 4½hrs), accommodation, refreshments; 66 places in dortoirs and beds; manned from June to mid-Sept (Tel 0165 86 90 97 info@rifugiomontebianco.com).

Here you come onto a road which is followed all the way into the Val Veni, with the Grandes Jorasses and Dent du Géant looking splendid ahead. About 25mins or so beyond the refuge the road is joined by another coming through the valley. Keep right, and 5mins later draw level with the little 19th-century chapel of **Notre Dame de la Guérison** (1444m, 4¾hrs) opposite the entrance to the Mont Blanc Tunnel.

Curving round the base of Mont Chétif, Val Veni is left behind and you enter the upper reaches of Val d'Aosta. When the road forks, with the left branch crossing the valley to La Saxe, keep on the right-hand option as far as **Entrélevie** (1226m, 5¼hrs). Now cross the river (the Doire Baltéa) and the main road, and turn right into Via dei Bagni which leads into

COURMAYEUR – see main route via Dolonne.

Main route to Courmayeur via Dolonne

Passing the rifugio bear right on a track/dirt road and shortly come to a junction of tracks where you walk ahead over grass, along the left-hand side of a ski lift, then down a piste towards buildings. On reaching a house bear left, and 10mins from Maison Vieille come to the

RIFUGIO LE RANDONNEUR (1890m) 25 dortoir places and beds; open from mid-June to end of Sept (Tel 349 53 68 898; info@randonneurmb.com; **www. randonneurmb.com**).

About 1min beyond this privately-owned gîte leave the main track for a minor one descending past a snack bar, and shortly after come to another ski tow where you descend timber-braced steps on a narrow path winding down grass slopes. This eventually brings you to another track/dirt road where you bear left and wander down towards the Funivia Courmayeur (cablecar station). Turn left on another track which takes you to the cableway building. To the left of this you will find a narrow signed footpath which descends steeply down a wooded slope and soon joins a crossing path. Turn right to continue the steep descent among trees. About 50mins from Col Chécrouit the path brings you onto a dirt road at a hairpin bend. Immediately turn left on a continuing path. Winding through more steep woodland eventually come onto a narrow tarmac lane just above **Dolonne** (1210m, 5¼hrs, *accommodation, refreshments*), an attractive stone-built village with crowded narrow streets.

Walk into the village along the Strada Chécrouit, and bear left into the main street (Via della Vittoria) where it crosses. Shortly before reaching the church a TMB sign directs the way to the right and this will lead out of Dolonne to the road linking the village with Courmayeur across the river. A splendid view shows the Aiguille (or Dent) du Géant soaring above the head of the valley. Walk down the road and across the river, and soon after go beneath the main road and out to a major junction, the Piazzale Monte Bianco, in **Courmayeur**

Should you need to cut short your TMB circuit here, buses run daily through the Mont Blanc Tunnel to Chamonix.

(13) which rises in tiers above you. Both the tourist office and post office are located in the large building ahead on the left. The bus station and public toilets are also on the left, while just ahead there's a drinking water supply and telephone kiosks. Check at the tourist office for accommodation. ◄

COURMAYEUR (1226m, 5½hrs) hotels, pensions, restaurants, banks, ATM, shops, PTT. Tourist information: AIAT Monte Bianco, Piazzale Monte Bianco 13, Courmayeur (Tel 01 65 84 20 60; courmayer@turismo. vda.it; **www.lovevda.it**). Lower-priced accommodation: Pensione Venezia (Tel 01 65 84 24 61); Hotel Select (Tel 01 65 84 66 61; select@courmayeurhotel.com; **www.courmayeurhotel.com**); Hotel Edelweiss (Tel 01 65 84 15 90; info@albergoedelweiss.it); Hotel Svizzero (Tel 01 65 84 81 70; info@hotelsvizzero.com; **www. hotelsvizzero.com**); Hotel Crampon (Tel 01 65 84 23 85 info@crampon.it; **www.crampon.it**).

A GOOD PLACE FOR A REST DAY

Despite the lively crowds who gather here, Courmayeur has a restful atmosphere, and with the soaring mountain walls blocking the northern horizon, it has an attraction all its own. 'All the great climbers of the Alps have been at Courmayeur,' wrote RLG Irving, 'and probably none has learned to climb there, except the many guides it has produced. It is a haven whence men set out for great adventures and return from them… The turning of the corner out of the deep trough below the great mountain wall, from whichever end of it you come [the Vals Veni or Ferret], brings you into a different world.'

If you plan to have a day off in Courmayeur and the weather is clear consider riding the **Funivie Monte Bianco** (cablecar) from La Palud to Point Helbronner at 3462m for tremendous high mountain views. You can then continue by gondola across 5km of the glaciated Vallée Blanche to the Aiguille du Midi (above Chamonix) and back again; a truly memorable experience.

STAGE 5
Courmayeur – Rifugio Bonatti

Start point	Courmayeur (1226m)
Distance	12km (16km or 14km via *variantes* 1 and 2
Height gain	860m (1597m or 1449m)
Height loss	101m (698m or 550m by the *variants*)
Time	4½hrs (6½–7hrs or 6–6½hrs via *variantes* 1 and 2)
High point	Tête de la Tronche (2584m) (Mont de la Saxe option)
Transport option	Bus (Courmayeur – Arnuva in Val Ferret – on Stage 6)
Accommodation	Le Pré (2hrs) – privately-owned refuge (Rifugio Bertone)
	Rifugio Bonatti – privately-owned refuge above La Vachey
Alternative route	Villair – Val Sapin – Col Sapin

In good conditions this stage promises to be one of the highlights of the Tour of Mont Blanc.

The grandeur of yesterday's views from the high route above Val Veni are matched on this stage along the flank of Mont (or Monte) de la Saxe where an easy, undulating path can be walked at leisure with eyes forever turning to the great wall of rock and ice across the Val Ferret. A few ruined huts tell of one-time alps; in early summer alpenroses colour the slopes with scarlet; in the autumn larches add a splash of yellow and gold. The stage is a delight from start to finish.

Until 2006 the TMB followed the Mont de la Saxe crest, regarded by many as the best viewpoint from which to study the south side of the Mont Blanc range. But the walker paid for that view with physical effort, for to reach the crest involves a steep and wearisome climb of more than 1200m out of Courmayeur. As Andrew Harper said in the predecessor to this guide: 'the visual prospects for the route … are spectacular'. That route is included here as an alternative to the newly rerouted TMB.

Another alternative option is to go through Val Sapin, which lies southeast of Mont de la Saxe, and join the main route at the col at its head. Beyond Col Sapin the way descends into the head of the Vallon d'Armina, climbs to the easy saddle of Pas Entre-Deux-Sauts and then drops into the Vallon de Malatra, on one of whose lower terraces stands the splendid Rifugio Bonatti, with a direct view of the Grandes Jorasses across the depths of Val Ferret.

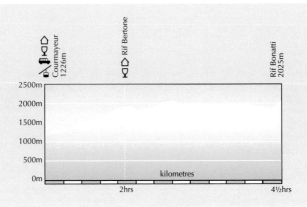

Begin the day's journey in the elevated square in front of the church and walk up the narrow street on its left (between the church and guides' office); this becomes the Strada del Villair. Keep on this road as it takes you out of Courmayeur alongside neat gardens and gently up a slope between houses to the upper part of **Villair** (1327m, 25mins), where the metalled road becomes unsurfaced. Continue along this unmade road to where it crosses a bridge and curves left. At the first right-hand hairpin, take a footpath on the left which soon brings you onto the road again. Cross directly ahead, eventually rejoining the

TMB VARIANTE: VAL SAPIN – COL SAPIN

Remain on the dirt road which pushes through Val Sapin on the west side of the stream, passing between the huddled buildings of **La Trappe** (1505m) and on to Chapy. A short distance beyond this cross the stream and climb the hillside heading south then east to be joined by another path coming from Courmayeur via La Suche. The way continues to the alp **Curru** (1964m, 2hrs 20mins). Col Sapin is now almost 500m above to the northeast, and the path to it cuts across the hillside, crosses the stream once more and climbs in numerous zigzags to reach **Col Sapin** (2436m, 3hrs 50mins), where it joins the Mont de la Saxe option – see box on page 76.

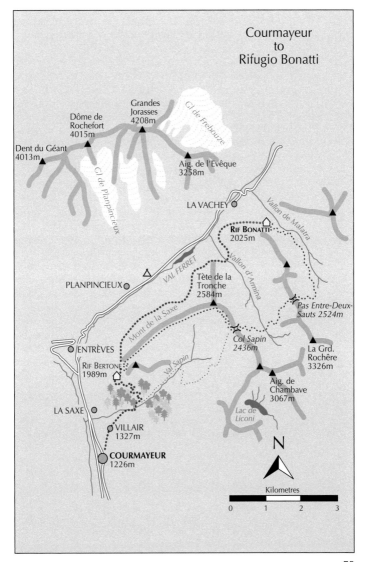

Courmayeur
to
Rifugio Bonatti

Dent du Géant
4013m

Dôme de
Rochefort
4015m

Grandes
Jorasses
4208m

Gl de Frébouze

Gl de Planpincieux

Aig. de l'Evêque
3258m

Vallon de Malatra

LA VACHEY

RIF BONATTI
2025m

Vallon d'Armina

VAL FERRET

PLANPINCIEUX

Mont de la Saxe

Tête de la
Tronche
2584m

Pas Entre-Deux-
Sauts 2524m

ENTRÈVES

Val Sapin

Col Sapin
2436m

La Grd.
Rochère
3326m

RIF BERTONE
1989m

Aig. de
Chambave
3067m

LA SAXE

*Lac de
Liconi*

VILLAIR
1327m

COURMAYEUR
1226m

N

Kilometres

0   1   2   3

road once more. Turn right along it. About 50 paces later the waymarked TMB path breaks off to the left (1460m, 45mins) and is signed to Rifugio Bertone.

Main TMB Route

Having left the unmade road the way climbs through forest and a few open patches, in places very steeply and with zigzags, but it's a well-made path and, taken at a steady, unhurried pace, can be most pleasant. From the point where you leave the road it will take 1–1¼hrs to reach the complex of stone buildings of Le Pré just above the treeline and dominated by the privately-owned

> **RIFUGIO GIORGIO BERTONE** (1989m, 2hrs) accommodation, refreshments; 55 dortoir places, 14 beds; open mid-June to end Sept (Tel 01 65 84 46 12; info@rifugiobertone.com; **www.rifugiobertone.it**).

Just below the rifugio a wonderful view is gained of Mont Blanc and the Aiguille Noire, as well as a bird's-eye view onto the toy-like buildings of Courmayeur, 700m below.

Continue above and to the right of the rifugio to reach a knoll at a junction with a path coming from the Val Ferret **(14)** to the left (c2030m). It is this path which now carries the route of the TMB, while the Mont de la Saxe ridge route continues above.

MONT DE LA SAXE OPTION

From the path junction climb steeply to gain the crest of Mont de la Saxe about 40mins later. From here, and all the way along the ridge to Tête de la Tronche, there's a stupendous panoramic view of the south wall of the Mont Blanc range from Col de la Seigne to the Grand Col Ferret, and in particular of the Grandes Jorasses seen across the valley to the north. (On 23 June 1865 Edward Whymper and his guides came here to study the mountain with a view to making its ascent, which they duly achieved next day. Unaccountably they went for the central summit instead of the main peak – Pointe Walker – which is only 24m higher.)

The wild south face of the Grande Jorasses seen from Mont de la Saxe

Passing avalanche fences the way leads along the grass crest heading northeast. In places the path unravels into several strands, and where it does, it's probably best to keep to the highest part of the ridge. Having passed just to the right of the 2534m Tête Bernarda a small saddle is reached, where a path drops to the left. Ignore this and keep on the TMB path, which slopes up towards the higher **Tête de la Tronche** on the right-hand side of the ridge. Come onto the high point of the walk at 2584m (4hrs), then descend to a notch looking onto the steep cliffs on the east side of the ridge. The path now descends very steeply (caution advised) to **Col Sapin** (2436m, 4¼–4½hrs).

Leaving the col the path descends a little north of east into the head of the tranquil Vallon d'Armina, reaching its lowest point where another path breaks away left (an 'escape route' down to La Vachey in Val Ferret). Ignore this option and contour across the floor of the cirque, crossing several streams on the way, then angle up the grass slope on the east side of the valley below Tête de Sécheron. About 1hr from Col Sapin reach the **Pas Entre-Deux-Sauts** (2524m, 5¼–5½hrs).

Descend into the head of the Vallon de Malatra on a gentle, meandering route over pastureland following a sometimes vague path below the slab face of the Grande Rochêre. Before long the path curves leftward with Mont Dolent and Aiguille de Triolet at first standing out ahead, then the Grandes Jorasses filling the view. Keep left of the main valley stream as you wander through a delightfully flat pasture, at the end of which you drop a little towards the buildings of Alpe supérieure de Malatra (2213m) and a junction of paths. Keep left and descend on a yellow waymarked path that soon breaks into several strands where the hillside has been cut by cattle. Make towards the left-hand side of more alp buildings (Malatra on the map), just below which you come to **Rifugio Bonatti (15)**.

Main TMB Route

At the path junction above Rifugio Bertone fork left to contour round the Val Ferret flank of Mont de la Saxe, gaining a magnificent view towards Col de la Seigne, with the Aiguille Noire, Mont Blanc and the Grandes Jorasses supporting a succession of glaciers, snowfields and abrupt rock walls. The path develops as a balcony trail among juniper, bilberry and thin larchwoods, then across open meadows with breathtaking views every step of the way. When the path forks above the ruins of Alp Leuchey (1938m; 2½hrs), continue ahead across pastureland, and 30mins later come to the long concrete cattle byre of Alp Lèche (1929m). The way now twists uphill, then angles across the hillside.

Turning a spur into the **Vallon d'Armina**, descend to the stream and cross on a sturdy timber footbridge, then go down towards the few buildings of Alp Arminaz (2033m) where the path suddenly turns right, climbs above a ruin, and joins another path (3½hrs). The TMB forks left to angle round the hillside on a gentle descent, soon among larchwoods before gaining Alp Sécheron. Pass directly above the buildings and continue ahead, coming to yet another junction (the last one of the day) about 20mins later. Turn right and briefly climb the slope to reach the well-appointed, privately-owned

RIFUGIO BONATTI (2025m, 4½hrs) accommodation, refreshments; 85 dortoir places; manned from March to April, and June to end of Sept (Tel 01 65 18 55 523; rifugiobonatti@gmail.com; **www.rifugiobonatti.it**).

Viewed from Rifugio Bonatti, Mont Blanc turns bronze with the sun's last glow

Should the rifugio be full, return to the path junction below the hut, and continue down the trail into the Val Ferret. Bear left and wander down the road to

LA VACHEY (1642m), about 1–1¼hrs from Rifugio Bonatti. Overnight accommodation may be had at the Hotel Lavachey, 21 beds; open mid-June to mid-Sept (Tel 01 65 86 97 23, **www.lavachey.com**).

STAGE 6
Rifugio Bonatti – Grand Col Ferret – La Fouly

Start point	Rifugio Bonatti (2025m)
Distance	20km
Height gain	895m
Height loss	1410m
Time	6–6½hrs
High point	Grand Col Ferret (2537m)
Transport options	Bus (La Vachey – Arnuva)
	Bus (Ferret – La Fouly)
Accommodation	Arnuva (1½hrs) – hotel
	Pré de Bar (2¼hrs) – refuge
	La Peule (4½-5hrs) – refuge
	Ferret (5¾–6hrs) – hotel
	La Léchère (6hrs) – gîte d'étape
	La Fouly – hotels, gîte, camping

The crossing of Grand Col Ferret takes the TMB out of Italy, into Switzerland and along the eastern edge of the Mont Blanc range. It's another fine route, for the day starts with a glorious contouring trail then descends into the Val Ferret, followed by an easy walk upvalley to Rifugio Elena, where the climb to the pass begins. This ascent is not too demanding under normal summer conditions, and will probably be no more taxing than the route to Col de la Seigne three days ago, while the way down into the Swiss Val Ferret on the far side is over rolling pastureland also without undue difficulties.

Among the highlights of this stage will undoubtedly be the view from the col looking back along the length of the Vals Ferret and Veni to the distant Col de la Seigne, a view partly framed by monstrous buttresses of rock. This will be the last sighting of the Grandes Jorasses for several days, for the next time this big block of mountain comes into view will be from the north, on the approach to La Flégère on Stage 10. The intimacy of the big mountains will be lost in the Swiss Val Ferret, although outliers of the range are seen – and seen to good effect – on the way to, and from, La Fouly. But this valley has other characteristics to enjoy: it has flower meadows and chalets with window boxes bursting with geraniums and petunias; it has milky streams, the clanging of cowbells, neat patches of forest and hamlets that appear to be untouched by passing centuries. Val Ferret lives up to its reputation as one of the most idyllic of Swiss valleys, and entry from the south enables the walker to make its acquaintance by stealth.

A short distance below the Grand Col Ferret a brief diversion from the main path leads to a view of the Swiss Val Ferret

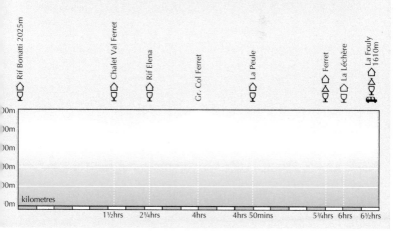

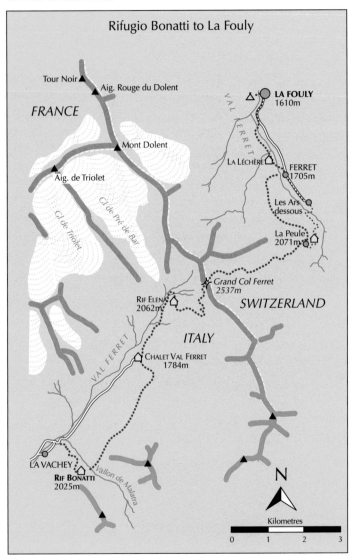

Rifugio Bonatti to La Fouly

Tour Noir
Aig. Rouge du Dolent
FRANCE
Mont Dolent
Aig. de Triolet
Gl de Triolet
Gl de Pré de Bar
VAL FERRET
LA FOULY
1610m
LA LÉCHÈRE
FERRET
1705m
Les Ars
dessous
La Peule
2071m
Grand Col Ferret
2537m
RIF ELENA
2062m
SWITZERLAND
ITALY
VAL FERRET
CHALET VAL FERRET
1784m
LA VACHEY
Vallon de Malatra
RIF BONATTI
2025m
N
Kilometres
0   1   2   3

Out of the rifugio go up the slope to the Malatra alp huts, and bear left on a path which makes a traverse of the hillside. Three streams are crossed, the second of which comes crashing over a series of cascades, but after the third stream crossing the path curves leftwards and slopes down to the derelict alp buildings of Gioé (2007m). Go between the buildings, and when the path forks keep straight ahead. Reaching a high point on a corner, 20mins from the rifugio, the path then slopes downhill with a fine view of the Pré-de-Bar glacier's big moraine wall ahead.

The hillside here is a delight of alpenrose, bilberry and larch, and views are exciting as the trail rises and falls towards the head of the Val Ferret, crossing several minor streams along the way. In a little over an hour you come to an alp building at a junction of paths. Bear left and descend to another fork where you keep ahead (the right-hand option), eventually reaching the valley floor by the small

CHALET VAL FERRET (1784m, 1½hrs) bar/restaurant, 14 beds; open June to end of Sept (Tel 01 65 84 49 59; info@chaletvalferret.com; **www.chaletvalferret.com**).

Walk along the tarmac approach road for about 100m, turn right to cross the river and follow the track to a parking area, on the far side of which a path carries the continuing TMB to Rifugio Elena and the Grand Col Ferret. The path climbs steeply in places, takes you past a group of ruins, crosses a stream on a footbridge, and then even more steeply up a slope to gain

RIFUGIO ELENA (2062m, 2¼hrs) accommodation, refreshments; 128 dortoir places, 15 beds; manned mid-June to mid-Sept (Tel 01 65 84 46 88; rifugioelena@virgilio.it).

The rifugio has been built into the hillside for protection – a wise precaution since the previous Elena hut was destroyed by avalanche in the 1950s. From it one looks across the valley onto the Glacier de Pré de Bar, which sweeps down from Mont Dolent. The upper névé basin of this glacier is rimmed by a ridge linking that multi-frontiered peak with Aiguille de Triolet; then two banks of rock squeeze the icefall before releasing it to spew the rounded snout into a wash of grey moraine debris. Because of its accessibility and easy viewing, and the refreshment facilities afforded by the Elena rifugio, the rather drab Pré de Bar glacier attracts hordes of visitors during the summer.

Two cols Ferret cross the frontier ridge above the Elena hut, but it is the southernmost (and higher) pass that is adopted by the TMB. Behind the hut the well-made and justifiably popular path turns away from the glacier and slants to the right across the hillside, then in a series of zigzags that lead up and past a few ruins. Beyond these the way angles up a little further before turning left and climbing steeply towards the pass. A little under 2hrs from the Elena rifugio, come onto the watershed of the **Grand Col Ferret** (2537m, 4hrs) for your first view into Switzerland, which is rather unprepossessing by contrast with the backward view. Only the snowy Grand Combin in the distance is worthy of attention to the east, but looking northwest along the frontier ridge Mont Dolent (16) is of interest, as is the Aiguille de Triolet to its left. However, it is the view back down through the Val Ferret to Val Veni and the distant Col de la Seigne that gives most value. An orientation table helps identify major points in the panorama.

Snow often lies on the Swiss side of the col well into the summer, where the gentle grass slopes are dipped with hollows and scoops. The way is invariably marked. At first veering left, then curving round to the east, about 8mins from the col note a minor (unmarked) path striking left ahead away from the main TMB. If you follow this a short distance it brings you to a wonderful viewpoint overlooking, through a dip in the grassy ridge, almost the full length of the Swiss Val Ferret.

Regaining the main path, the way angles across broad open slopes which sweep down into the combe of Revers de la Peule. The path keeps high above this, however, and about 50mins after leaving the col it brings you to the summer dairy farm of

ALPAGE DE LA PEULE (2071m, 4hrs 50mins) accommodation, refreshments; 30 places in dorms and yurts; open in summer (Tel 027 783 10 44; coppey. lapeule@dransnet.ch; **www.lapeulaz.skyrock.com**).

Looking back on the high trail between La Peule and Ferret

The TMB formerly continued its descent into the Val Ferret by following the farm road all the way from La Peule. This has now become a *variante*, an easy walk described in the box below. The main TMB now takes a higher and more scenic route, contouring along the hillside before descending steeply to the valley between Ferret and the gîte La Léchère. If visibility is poor, or there's heavy rain, take the *variante*. Otherwise the main route is highly recommended.

Main TMB Route
At the first alp building of La Peule turn sharp left onto a narrow path cutting across the pastures. This is signed to Ferret and La Léchère. After contouring for a while, the trail turns a spur among bilberries to gain a tremendous view of Mont Dolent, Tour Noir and their glaciers, with the Val Ferret stretching to the north. Now sloping downhill,

TMB VARIANTE

From La Peule take the unsurfaced farm road that winds downhill, and after about 30mins cross a bridge spanning the Drance de Ferret at about 1775m. Walk up the slope to another road just below the dairy farm of Les Ars dessous where a *buvette* serves refreshments (5hrs 25mins). Walk down the road for about 20mins to reach the little hamlet of

FERRET (1705m, 5¾-6hrs) accommodation, refreshments; buses via La Fouly to Champex and Orsières. Accommodation at Hotel Col de Fenêtre: 18 dortoir places, 17 beds; open June to end Sept (Tel 027 783 11 88, bertrandmurisier@bluewin.ch).

For the continuing route to La Fouly, immediately before coming to the first of Ferret's buildings, take a path on the left which descends to a footbridge spanning the river. Over this turn right on a riverside trail and wander downstream through light woodland. On reaching a more substantial bridge over a side stream, you rejoin the main TMB.

cross a narrow gully, then rise again. About 40mins from La Peule enter the combe of Les Creuses (headed by the Tête de Ferret) where you come to a low concrete hut and a footpath sign directing the way downhill to La Léchère.

Descend to a glade of larches, below which there's a junction of paths (about 15mins from the concrete hut). The right-hand path is the one to take if you need accommodation or refreshments at **Ferret**, which you can see below on the right bank of the Drance de Ferret. The left-hand option descends very steeply to a substantial footbridge spanning the stream draining the Creuses combe. It is here that the alternative route from La Peule rejoins the main TMB.

Cross the bridge, and 5mins later note a narrow signed path cutting up the left-hand hillside to the

GÎTE DE LA LÉCHÈRE (6hrs) accommodation, refreshments; 35 dortoir places; open June to end Sept (Tel 079 433 49 78; www.lalechere.ch).

Unless you plan to visit La Léchère continue ahead and follow a track ahead which is joined by another soon after.

The tiny chapel at Ferret

Rising a little and turning a bend, pass a building where a signpost directs the TMB path to the right, dropping through a sloping meadow and into trees. Through these you come to a bridge over the river. Cross to the road and turn left. A few minutes later enter the small village of **La Fouly (17)**, with its glorious outlook west into a cirque of mountains crowned by Mont Dolent and the Tour Noir.

> **LA FOULY** (1610m, 6½hrs) hotels, gîte, camping, supermarket, ATM, restaurants, PTT, buses to Orsières and Champex; tourist office (Tel 027 775 23 84; **www. lafouly.ch/en**). Lower-priced accommodation: Chalet Le Dolent, 65 dortoir places, 10 beds, open all year (Tel 027 783 29 31; info@dolent.ch; **www.dolent.ch**); Gîte Les Girolles, 60 beds, open all year (Tel 027 783 18 75; lesgirolles@netplus.ch); Auberge des Glaciers, 34 dortoir places, 22 beds, open June to October (Tel 027 783 11 71; info@aubergedesglaciers.ch); Hotel Edelweiss, 25 dortoir places, 45 beds, open end of May to end of Sept (Tel 027 783 26 21, hotel.edelweiss@ st-bernard.ch).

STAGE 7
La Fouly – Champex

Start point	La Fouly (1610m)
Distance	15km
Height gain	420m
Height loss	565m
Time	4–4½hrs
High point	Champex (1466m)
Transport options	Bus (La Fouly – Champex)
Accommodation	Champex – hotels, pensions, gîte, camping
	Val d'Arpette (+ 45mins Alt. Stage 8) – hotel/dortoir, camping
	Champex d'en Haut (+ 30mins Stage 8) – hotel, gîte

This is the easiest stage of the TMB, and with a modest amount of height gain and loss the day can be taken at a leisurely pace. With neither passes to cross nor high and remote country to traverse, it's a valley walk throughout. But that is not to say it's without interest. On the contrary: here we experience the pastoral nature of a Swiss mountain valley, where the way of life of the local farming communities appears at first glance to have been barely touched by modern technology. As Walt Unsworth commented in his account of the TMB in *Classic Walks of the World*: 'the old ways still carry weight, and it seems appropriate somehow that in this slightly unreal world the chief produce should be strawberries'. Elsewhere dairy cattle graze the pastures, meadows lie striped behind the scythe, and the old dark-timbered barns send out the rich fragrance of warm hay. For the most part, glacier-hung mountains are hidden from view.

Walk through the village along the road as far as the Grand Hotel du Val Ferret, where a footpath descends on the left among larches, crosses a track and continues across the river by a sluice. Turn right on a service road, and about 120m later bear right on a continuing TMB track through woodland. About 15mins from La Fouly cross a meadow below the 400m high Amône Slab on

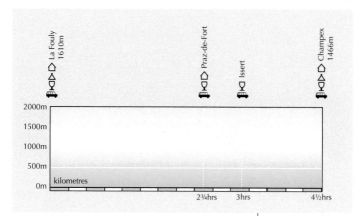

which climbers can sometimes be seen in action. A track swings right here to cross the river, but we keep ahead and in another 20mins or so come to a junction of tracks in a clearing where one route cuts off to the right and is signed to Prayon.

Ignoring this alternative, keep ahead where the track gently loses height to another fork by a bridge at 1370m. About 10mins later leave the track at a hairpin where a signed footpath soon rises along the wooded hillside, and after a while comes to an open, slightly exposed section safeguarded with a fixed chain, then continues among trees, descending at first with zigzags, then less steeply.

Approaching the as yet unseen Saleina tributary, the TMB turns right at a signed junction onto the ancient lateral moraine of the fast-receding Saleina glacier. This is the Crête de Saleina, a wooded causeway topped by a good path which follows the crest for several minutes before sloping downhill to a dirt road near a bridge. Bear left, and keep ahead when the road becomes metalled, then cross the mouth of the tributary valley. Remain on the road between chalets, cross the Reuse de Saleina and take the right branch when it forks. The TMB now slopes gently downhill, passing the old houses and barns of

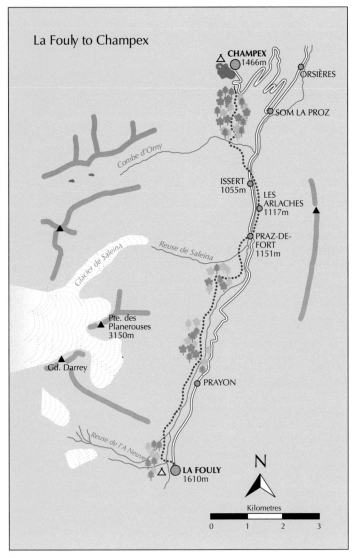

La Fouly to Champex

△ **CHAMPEX**
1466m

ORSIÈRES

SOM LA PROZ

Combe d'Orny

ISSERT
1055m

LES
ARLACHES
1117m

PRAZ-DE-
FORT
1151m

Reuse de Saleina

Glacier de Saleina

Pte. des
Planerouses
3150m

Gd. Darrey

PRAYON

Reuse de l'A Neuve

△ **LA FOULY**
1610m

N

Kilometres

0   1   2   3

PRAZ-DE-FORT (1151m, 2hrs) refreshments, PTT, grocery.

Turn right on the main road, cross the river then bear left on the waymarked route through meadows leading in another 10mins to the charming little hamlet of **Les Arlaches** (1117m). Keep ahead through this hamlet, with its timeless chalets and barns crowded one against another, after which the next village, Issert, can be seen ahead astride the main road a little under 10mins walk away. The main track leads down to the road on the village outskirts, but the TMB cuts off to the right at a T-junction on an alternative track which crosses a bridge in the centre of **Issert** (1055m, 2½hrs, *refreshments*).

Turn right along the main road, and about 100m beyond the last buildings a signpost directs the TMB left (Champex 1½hrs) along a lane, over a stream, up a track, then on a footpath which soon enters forest. After 2½hrs of walking mostly downhill or along the flat since La Fouly,

An old flower-adorned house in Issert

the prospect of a 1½hr climb to Champex comes as something of a shock. In truth the ascent is modest by comparison with much that has gone before, so you should settle into a comfortable stride and enjoy this mostly forested walk. There are numerous path junctions, but the way is either obvious or waymarked with a yellow diamond outlined in black. The route has been adopted as the Sentier des Champignons, and is decorated with a number of wood carvings that include mushrooms, squirrels, an eagle and so on. After about 3½hrs the path brings you above two small chalets where, on a bend, there's a water supply, picnic table and a bird's-eye view onto Orsières. As you draw close to Champex the TMB brings you to the road linking Orsières with Champex. Cross with care, bear left and rounding a bend take a signed footpath rising above the road. This takes you through woodland before coming onto a minor service road near Hotel Bellevue. A few paces before the hotel, cross an open space on the left to join another service road. Turn left and shortly after you will arrive at the southeastern end of **Champex (18)**.

CHAMPEX (1466m, 4–4½hrs) hotels, pensions, gîte, camping; restaurants, shops, PTT, tourist information (Tel 027 775 23 83, champexlac@saint-bernard.ch; www. champex.info). Lower-priced accommodation: Pension En Plein Air, 48 dortoir places, 25 beds, open all year (Tel 027 783 23 50; pensionenpleinair@bluewin.ch); Au Club Alpin, 25 dortoir places, open all year (Tel 027 783 11 61); Chalet du Jardin Alpin, 8 dortoir places, 13 beds, self-catering only, open May to end Oct (Tel 027 783 12 17; info@flore-alpe.ch); Camping Les Rocailles, open all year (Tel 027 783 19 79), is located at the top end of the village. Other accommodation options lie on the route of Stage 8 (+ 30mins) and Alternative Stage 8 (+ 45mins). Refer to the appropriate sections for details.

STAGE 8
Champex – Alp Bovine – Col de la Forclaz

Start point	Champex (1466m)
Distance	16km
Height gain	742m
Height loss	682m
Time	4½–5hrs
High point	Collet Portalo (2040m)
Transport option	Postbus and train (Champex – Orsières – Martigny – Forclaz)
Accommodation	Champex d'en Haut (30mins) – gîte, hotel
	Bovine (3¼hrs) – emergency dortoir only
	Col de la Forclaz – hotel/dortoir, camping
	Trient (+ 30mins) – dortoirs
	Le Peuty (+ 45mins) – gîte, camping
Alternative route	Champex – Fenêtre d'Arpette – Forclaz (see Alternative Stage 8)

The Fenêtre d'Arpette route to Col de la Forclaz – Alternative Stage 8 – is a much tougher, but more spectacular option that should only be considered if the forecast is for calm, settled weather.

The stage described here is the easier of the two routes to Col de la Forclaz; an undulating walk that makes a loop round the northern slopes of a rocky spur projecting, in essence, from the Pointe d'Orny. Study of the IGN map shows the rumpled nature of this route. It curves, dips and rises over unsettled contours and in and out of indents in the hillside. There are neat meadows, patches of forest, rough combes and high alpine pastures leading to the simple alp buildings of Bovine, which look down onto Martigny in the Rhône valley and across to mountains of the Bernese Alps.

Refreshments and emergency accommodation are available at the Bovine alp, while the hotel at Col de la Forclaz provides two-tier accommodation with bedrooms and dormitories, and facilities for campers too. Accommodation is also available in Trient, a small village in the valley below and to the west of Forclaz, and at nearby Le Peuty, both of which are on one of the optional TMB routes of Stage 9.

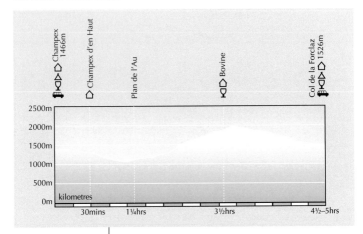

Walk up the road leading out of Champex, passing the campsite on your right and, above this, the La Breya chairlift on the left. Continue for a few more minutes, then turn left at a junction on a minor road. About 20mins after leaving Champex pass the Bon-Abri gîte, seen to the right. This is part of the small community of

CHAMPEX D'EN HAUT (1440m, 20mins) accommodation: Chalet Bon-Abri, 33 dortoir places, 42 beds, open all year (Tel 027 783 14 23, contact@ gite-bonabri.com; **www.gite-bonabri.com**); Hotel-Club Sunways, 77 beds, open Dec to April and June to Sept (Tel 027 783 11 22; hotel@sunways.ch).

When the road forks branch right to descend to a lower road at a four-way junction. Turn left and soon pass the string of chalets at **Champex d'en Bas** (1340m) in another 15mins, below which open meadows make this a very pleasant stretch to wander along. At the far end of the meadows turn left on a track where a sign indicates the way to Plan de l'Au and Bovine. After passing a few chalets a footpath leads through woodland and out to a narrow metalled road. Turn left and 2mins later come to the

94

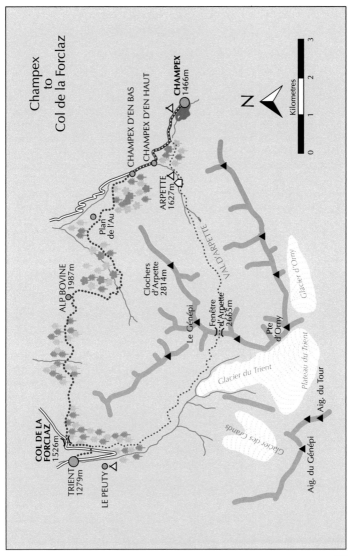

Champex to Col de la Forclaz

farm buildings of **Plan de l'Au** (1330m, 1¼hrs, *refreshments*) with a view into the Rhône valley.

From here the road is an unsurfaced 4x4 track rising steadily for another 20mins or so, after which it curves left at a gateway and narrows to a footpath. ◄ The original TMB now climbs into the wooded combe of La Jure. There are several streams to cross, and as you gain height the vegetation changes, with bilberries lining the steep and rocky path. High above, a craggy ridge links the Clochers d'Arpette with Le Génepi.

Having climbed above tree level the way curves right (north), crosses a final stream and angles gently across an open slope. On a clear day the snowy mass of the Grand Combin can be seen to the southeast, the Dents du Midi to the northwest, and steeply below the Rhône valley runs a straight furrow below the range of the Bernese Alps. Turning a spur of the Pointe Ronde, the path now curves west to gain a first sighting of the buildings of

ALP BOVINE (1987m, 3¼hrs, emergency dortoir accommodation, refreshments).

Alp Bovine is located on a gentle slope of pasture facing northeast along the Rhône valley, providing a contrast between the pastoral life of the traditional alp farmer and the modern, high-tech agriculturalist with his orchards and vineyards 1500m below. Bovine is a working dairy farm, but the farmer's income is supplemented by refreshments served to passing walkers. Simple dortoir accommodation may be available here.

Although this is not the highest point of the walk, most of the day's demands are now over, for there's only a short rise of just 53m to achieve beyond the alp buildings, where the path leads up to a gate in a fence on the edge of larch and pinewoods a few minutes' walk away. This is the so-called **Collet Portalo** (2040m, 3½hrs). Pause for a moment to enjoy a last view back to the Grand Combin. Once through the gate the pleasant woodland path is mostly downhill to Col de la Forclaz, passing on the way another group of alp buildings (La Giète 1884m)

In the summer of 2012 a new path was created which now makes a more gently graded ascent to Alp Bovine. Sadly it misses some really attractive sections enjoyed by the 'original' route which still exists and is described here.

The Bovine alp, with the Grand Combin in the distance floating among the clouds

on the left. The trail is often greasy in places, with some steeply descending sections. On occasion a brief view is gained through the trees to Martigny on a bend in the Rhône valley, and of the road which snakes its way up through the Martigny Combe to Forclaz.

At last the path emerges from woodland with the **Col de la Forclaz (19)** just ahead.

COL DE LA FORCLAZ (1526m, 4½–5hrs) refreshments, shop, bus to Martigny and Trient, accommodation in Hotel du Col de la Forclaz, 40 dortoir places, 35 beds, camping, open mid-Dec to Nov (Tel 027 722 26 88; colforclazhotel@bluewin.ch; **www.coldelaforclaz.ch**).

Note Dortoir accommodation is also available in Trient (+ 30mins) and Le Peuty – also camping (+ 45mins) in the Vallée du Trient below to the west. See Stage 9 below for details.

ALTERNATIVE STAGE 8
Champex – Fenêtre d'Arpette – Col de la Forclaz

Start point	Champex (1466m)
Distance	14km
Height gain	1199m
Height loss	1139m
Time	6½hrs
High point	Fenêtre d'Arpette (2665m)
Accommodation	Arpette (45mins) – hotel/dortoir, camping
	Le Peuty (6¼hrs) – gîte, camping
	Trient (6½hrs) – dortoirs
	Les Grands (7hrs) – CAS refuge
	Col de la Forclaz – hotel/dortoir, camping
Alternative route	Champex – Bovine – Col de la Forclaz (see Stage 8)

A note of warning before setting out: the crossing should not be attempted other than in good conditions and with a forecast of settled weather. In the event of neither of these provisos being met, you are advised to use Stage 8, the 'Bovine' route described above.

Along with Col des Fours (see *variante* on Stage 2), which shares the same altitude, the Fenêtre d'Arpette is the highest point reached on the Tour of Mont Blanc, and its crossing from Champex is the toughest of the whole route. The statistics of height gain and loss provide a clue as to its strenuous nature, but the reality of this will only be felt on the final approach to the pass where, after negotiating a chaos of boulders, a steep slope of grit ensures that your arrival at the Fenêtre is cause for relief. That being said, the Fenêtre d'Arpette is a true mountain pass and one to enjoy for the sudden extraordinary vision of the upper Trient glacier revealed as you emerge through the western side. That glacier is on display for most of the descent – that and a long view to the north, which together make the route down one of great beauty.

At the foot of the pass there's a choice of routes to consider. The easiest is to follow a near-level bisse path to the Col de la Forclaz. Or you could shorten Stage 9 by crossing the glacial torrent below the Chalet du Glacier and climbing for 1½hrs to Refuge Les Grands (self-catering accommodation only) or, across the torrent, go down to Le Peuty (30mins) or Trient (45mins). These various options are described in detail below.

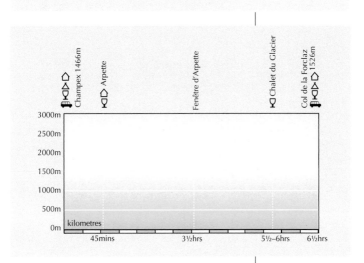

Leaving Champex walk up the road to pass the campsite on the right, and shortly after this turn left at a hairpin bend by a café-restaurant into a narrow road (direction Val d'Arpette). Very shortly a signpost directs the TMB to the right, passes beneath a chairlift by a small pond and enters woods. The path joins a *bisse* (irrigation channel), and when it forks you take the left branch, a good contouring path with a fine view through the valley to the right to the distant Dents du Midi. The way continues along the hillside through a forest of spruce and fir with the bisse for company, and on coming to a diversion weir, climbs up to a road where you turn right and shortly draw level with the

RELAIS D'ARPETTE (1627m, 45mins) refreshments, 86 dortoir places, 14 beds, camping, open May to end of Oct (Tel 027 783 12 21; info@arpette.ch).

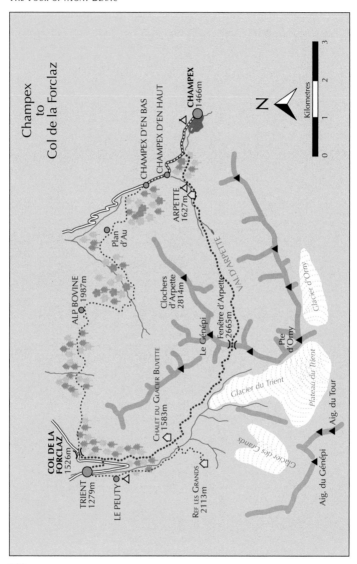

Champex
to
Col de la Forclaz

CHAMPEX
1466m

CHAMPEX D'EN BAS

CHAMPEX D'EN HAUT

ARPETTE
1627m

Plan
d'Au

VAL D'ARPETTE

Clochers
d'Arpette
2814m

ALP BOVINE
1987m

Le Génépi

Fenêtre d'Arpette
2665m

Glacier d'Orny

Pte
d'Orny

CHALET DU GLACIER BUVETTE
1583m

COL DE LA
FORCLAZ
1526m

Glacier du Trient

Plateau du Trient

Aig. du Tour

TRIENT
1279m

LE PEUTY

REF LES GRANDS
2113m

Glacier des Grands

Aig. du Génépi

Kilometres

0   1   2   3

Beyond the hotel the road is unmade, and after passing some chalets overlooking the valley meadows, is no longer drivable. Continue along the ensuing track from which the Val d'Arpette (**20**) grows increasingly attractive, and about 30–35mins from the hotel reach a signpost indicating the way to the Fenêtre d'Arpette on a footpath to the right.

At first among trees, this narrow path dodges to and fro across a stream until coming to a more open region, where it begins to climb in earnest through a steep and narrow area. At the top of this bear right at a path junction. The Fenêtre d'Arpette now comes into view as the lowest cut in a skyline crest to the right of some dark spiky crags. The way continues to climb on the north flank of the valley towards its wild upper reaches, and eventually brings you to a chaos of boulders, across which you fight a way to the foot of the final slope. Waymarks and small cairns lead the way across these boulders, but they are not always clearly visible. Great care needs to be taken on this section, for some of the boulders are unstable.

Once across the boulders a steep, gritty slope now rises ahead. Snow patches often lie across this right through the summer, and the path has numerous strands to it. Allow 20–30mins for this final climb, and enjoy a good rest when you arrive at last on the **Fenêtre d'Arpette** (2665m, 3½–4hrs).

Descending the western side of the Fenêtre – almost as steep as the Arpette side

101

THE FENÊTRE D'ARPETTE

The Fenêtre is a highlight of the tour in every sense, a window – as its name suggests – onto a new landscape, and is one to savour. The west side of the ridge looks onto the tumbling Trient glacier, spilling its way from the great Plateau du Trient, a 'sweeping snow lake' as it was described by Emile Javelle (in *Souvenirs d'un Alpiniste*). The glacier, now shrinking fast, has carved out a deep valley, the Vallée du Trient (**21**), which lies far below, and into which the descending path will take you. But when you look back the way you've come,

the scene contrasts markedly with that ahead. Here one gazes across a vast slope of scree to bold ridges funnelling the view east and southeast to where the glaciers and snowfields of the Combin massif block the horizon.

The eastern side of the Fenêtre

Through the upthrusting rocks which guard the Fenêtre the marked route swings to the right and descends across a jumble of rocks (caution advised) before settling to a good path that loops down towards the right-hand lateral moraine of the Trient glacier. As mentioned above, this is shrinking fast and now terminates at its icefall, revealing ice-smoothed slabs below where in recent years the glacier lay deep. In places the path drops steeply, then eases to pass the low ruins of Vésevey (2096m). Not long after passing these you come to the first trees, and about 2hrs from the Fenêtre arrive at the *buvette* known as the **Chalet du Glacier** (1583m, 5½–6hrs, *refreshments*). A few paces beyond this you'll find a path junction.

Before going further a decision needs to be made in regard to your overnight accommodation. Possibilities are:

- Hotel du Col de la Forclaz (in 45mins) – beds and dortoirs
- Refuge Les Grands – no meals provision (1½hrs)
- Le Peuty for gîte and camping (30mins) and Trient (45mins) for dortoirs.

Much, of course, will depend on your state of fitness after the demands of the route so far. But you'll also need to consider tomorrow's route too, for there's more than one way to reach the Col de Balme on Stage 9. All of the above overnight options are on one route or another to the col, except the Forclaz hotel. Walkers choosing to spend the night there will either return to this junction at Chalet du Glacier or descend to the road near Trient and walk back upvalley. Details will be found under Stage 9.

Route to Col de la Forclaz
Do not cross the torrent, but keep ahead along the easy, near-level path which accompanies the Bisse du Trient **(22)** for about 45mins all the way to the

HOTEL DU COL DE LA FORCLAZ (1526m, 6½hrs) refreshments, shop, bus to Martigny and Trient, accommodation; 40 dortoir places, 35 beds, camping, open mid-Dec to Nov (Tel 027 722 26 88; colforclazhotel@-bluewin.ch; **www.coldelaforclaz.ch**).

Route to Refuge Les Grands
Bear left at the signpost below the Chalet du Glacier, cross the footbridge and turn left on a good path which rises along the wooded hillside. When the path forks take the upper option (the alternative leads to the Alpage des Petoudes). Shortly after this junction the gradient steepens, and the path climbs in zigzags up the west side of the narrow valley falling from the Glacier des Grands. At the top of the zigzags the way slants to the right and crosses a shelf (safeguarded with fixed cable) against an impressive rock slab, and just above this comes to the

Refuge Les Grands, a simple but atmospheric place in which to spend a night

REFUGE LES GRANDS (2113m, 7–7½hrs) 15 dortoir places, cooking facilities, water supply, infrequently wardened (no meals provision); open mid-June to mid-Oct; for reservations (Tel 026 660 65 04).

Route to Le Peuty and Trient
Cross the footbridge below Chalet du Glacier and turn right on the path which slopes downhill, then onto a narrow tarmac road where you bear left. Before long a footpath on the right enables you to shortcut the road before rejoining it lower down. Now walk along this road across the mouth of the little Nant Noir valley to reach

LE PEUTY (1328m, 6–6½hrs) accommodation at the gîte Refuge Du Peuty: 37 dortoir places, no meals; open mid-June to mid-Sept (Tel 027 722 09 38); camping nearby.

Continue down the road for a further 10mins to reach

TRIENT (1279m, 6¼–6¾hrs) refreshments, food store, accommodation at: Auberge Mont Blanc, 60 dortoir places, 20 beds, open all year (Tel 027 767 15 05; info@aubergemontblanc.com); La Grande Ourse, 38 dortoir places, 18 beds, plus apartments, open all year (Tel 027 722 17 54; **www.la-grande-ourse.ch**).

STAGE 9

Col de la Forclaz – Col de Balme – Tré-le-Champ

Start point	Col de la Forclaz (1526m)
Distance	13km
Height gain	1069m
Height loss	1178m
Time	5½hrs
High point	Aiguillette des Posettes (2201m)
Accommodation	Le Peuty (30mins) – gîte, camping
	Col de Balme (3hrs) – refuge
	Tré-le-Champ – auberge/gîte
Alternative route	Col de la Forclaz – Les Grands – Col de Balme (see Alternative Stage 9)

Although the accumulated height gain and loss might suggest otherwise, this is not a particularly arduous stage, for the climb to Col de Balme, which accounts for the lion's share of ascent, is mostly achieved at a reasonably benevolent angle, although the second half of the descent from Aiguillette des Posettes is on a steep path that can aggravate tired legs.

Col de la Forclaz marks the northern extent of the TMB, the furthest point from the summit of Mont Blanc, but this stage carries the route over the final mountain barrier and returns it to the Vallée de l'Arve, which flows at the foot of the Monarch of the Alps. As it does, so Mont Blanc reappears, the first time since leaving Rifugio Bonatti at the start of Stage 6. Col de Balme, across which runs the Franco–Swiss border, provides the first view, and the lovely snow dome remains in sight for most of the descent to Tré-le-Champ. This is achieved along the crest of the Aiguillette des Posettes, an elevated path with a huge panorama.

Cross the road in front of Hotel du Col de la Forclaz and follow the path of the Bisse du Trient signed to Chalet du Glacier and Le Peuty. After 8mins take a steeply descending path that twists down the steep wooded slope and brings you over the road on a footbridge. Turn right and 40m later bear left on a track descending to Trient and

From Trient Simply walk up the lower, minor road below the village church for about 15mins to reach Le Peuty.

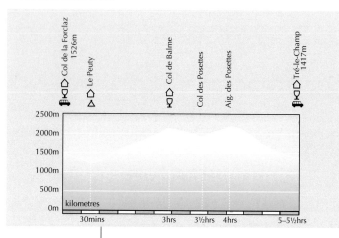

LE PEUTY (1328m, 30mins) accommodation at the gîte Refuge Du Peuty: 37 dortoir places; open mid-June to mid-Sept (Tel 027 722 09 38); camping nearby.

Immediately south of Refuge Du Peuty veer right on a track signed to Col de Balme, and cutting across the meadows fanning out at the mouth of the Vallon de Nant Noir. On crossing the Nant Noir stream the track becomes a footpath which enters woodland, then climbs in steep zigzags up the south flank of the valley. Eventually the gradient eases and you head to the right across a more open hillside to the old hutments of Herbagères (2036m, 2½hrs) in a rough hollow. From here the path goes up again with more zigzags to mount the final 150m or so to reach the

REFUGE DU COL DE BALME (2191m, 3hrs) accommodation, refreshments; 26 dortoir places (Tel 04 50 54 02 33).

The refuge enjoys a privileged position on the broad grassy saddle of the Col de Balme **(23)**, which carries the frontier between Switzerland and France. At the col itself two signs give conflicting altitudes: one says 2191m, the

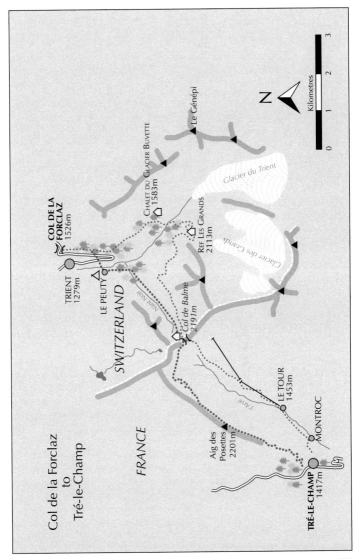

Col de la Forclaz
to
Tré-le-Champ

The Aiguilles Verte and Drus demand your attention at the Col de Balme

other 2204m. There has been a hostelry of some kind here for well over a century, a bone of contention between the two countries, as a result of which it has been burnt down and rebuilt several times. Purchases can be made at the refuge in either Swiss francs or Euros, while the views are magical.

Note The main route to Tré-le-Champ described below via the Aiguillette des Posettes should not be taken if there is any likelihood of storm. The alternative option is to descend directly from Col de Balme to Le Tour, and thence to Tré-le-Champ by the former TMB path (see box below).

Main Route via Aiguillette des Posettes

Go round to the right (north side) of the refuge and take the path which veers left, crosses onto the French slope and angles round to the right below the Tête de Balme before descending to a farm track and the open saddle of **Col des Posettes** (1997m, 3½hrs), where there's a multi-junction of paths and a signpost. A track breaks away right to Vallorcine; half-left ahead a

ALTERNATIVE TMB: COL DE BALME – LE TOUR – TRÉ-LE-CHAMP

Go to the left (south) of the refuge, then veer right at a signpost to descend a good path cutting down the centre of the slope to the middle station of a gondola lift at

CHARAMILLON (1850m), refreshments, accommodation nearby at the Gîte d'Alpage (Les Ecuries de Charamillon), 20 places, open mid-June to mid-Sept (Tel 04 50 54 17 07).

Beyond the lift station continue down to the valley station at

LE TOUR (1453m, 4hrs 20mins), accommodation in Chalet Alpin du Tour [CAF gîte] 87 places, open April to mid-Sept (Tel 04 50 54 04 16).

Le Tour is an attractive little village, the highest in the Chamonix valley. From here walk down the road to **Montroc** (1354m), which you reach in about 18mins, then cut off along a signed path on the right which crosses the railway tunnel and rises to **Tré-Le-Champ** (1417m) in another 15–20mins – a little over 2hrs from Col de Balme.

shorter low-level route goes to Tré-le-Champ and Col des Montets (*refreshments* at the Chalets de Balme). We, however, go straight ahead up a grass slope to pass above a ski tow, making for the crown of the Aiguillette des Posettes. The path has numerous braidings and the slope can be muddy in places where cattle have been grazing, but the way becomes rockier towards the top of the slope.

On gaining the crest the panoramic views are among the best of the walk. There is the rock-cradled Lac d'Emosson off to the right, restrained by its huge dam; the exquisite Aiguille du Chardonnet, Glacier du Tour, Aiguilles Verte and Drus, and the snow dome of Mont Blanc to focus one's gaze ahead and to the left, while alpine flowers and low-growing shrubs occupy crevices in the rocks or claw their way over them.

The path is a good one; it passes the cairn marking the summit of **L'Aiguillette des Posettes** (2201m, 4hrs) half an hour or so after leaving the signpost at the col, then begins the descent. From here to where the route enters forest, the path descends hundreds of timber-braced steps – caution when wet.

About 4–5mins below the Aiguillette come to a junction where the left-hand path angles down to Le Tour. Ignore this and continue ahead, soon descending in zigzags among alpenrose, bilberry and juniper. There are several other path junctions between here and the road below Col des Montets, and at each one you take the right-hand option. The path enters forest and twists its way down to a final T-junction of paths (1435m) a few paces above the road. Turn left here and walk downhill parallel with the road, soon emerging from the trees by a pair of old stone buildings and a small chapel. In another 100m take a stony jeep track sloping downhill on the left, leading to the hamlet of **Tré-le-Champ**.

> **TRÉ-LE-CHAMP** (1417m, 5–5½hrs) accommodation at the charming gîte Auberge la Boerne: 32 dortoir places, open all year (Tel 04 50 54 05 14; contact@la-boerne.fr; **www.la-boerne.fr**).

Note Should the Auberge be full, the nearest alternative accommodation is at the next hamlet, Les Frasserands (1360m, 15mins) – take the path which descends below Tré-le-Champ. Turn right at a narrow road in the hamlet, then left and follow down to a T-junction. Opposite stands the comfortable gîte Le Moulin, 38 dortoir places, open Dec to end of Sept; (Tel 04 50 54 05 37; benoit.henry2@wanadoo.fr; www.gite-chamonix.com).

A second option is to continue downvalley to Argentière (25mins) by taking the path which accompanies the stream outside the gîte in Tré-le-Champ. Argentière has hotels, a gîte (Le Belvédère), shops, restaurants, PTT, tourist information and bus service to Col des Montets.

ALTERNATIVE STAGE 9

Col de la Forclaz – Refuge Les Grands –
Tré-le-Champ

Start point	Col de la Forclaz (1526m)
Distance	18km
Height gain	869m
Height loss	978m
Time	6hrs
High points	Col de Balme 2191m and Aiguillette des Posettes 2201m
Accommodation	Les Grands (2¼hrs) – CAS refuge (no meals)
	Col de Balme (3¾–4hrs) – refuge
	Tré-le-Champ – auberge/gîte
Alternative route	Col de la Forclaz – Col de Balme direct (see Stage 9)

This TMB *variante* is, in some ways, a better and more varied route than the traditional stage through the Vallon de Nant Noir, although it's more strenuous than at first appears.

The day begins gently enough by following the Bisse du Trient along the wooded hillside to the Chalet du Glacier, then across the glacial torrent to a steep climb leading to the refuge at Les Grands. Above the refuge the path is almost frustratingly undulating – just as you think you've gained sufficient height to be almost at the same altitude as Col de Balme, the way descends, only to climb again. And so it goes on. That having been said, it's a scenic walk across ever-varied terrain, and one less travelled than the standard route. The two ways converge on the Col de Balme.

From the hotel at Col de la Forclaz cross the road and follow the signed path (Chalet du Glacier) which soon joins the Bisse du Trient (22) flowing south along the hillside through woodland. About halfway to Chalet du Glacier a clearing allows an unrestricted view through the Vallon de Nant Noir to the refuge on the Col de Balme. After about 45mins you should arrive at the path junction a few paces before the **Chalet du Glacier** (1583m, *refreshments*).

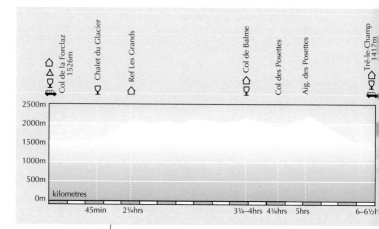

Descend to a footbridge spanning the torrent, from which you catch a view up to the Glacier du Trient, and on the far side turn left on a crossing path. This rises along the wooded hillside, gaining height steadily, and then forks. Take the upper path (the alternative leads round to the Alpage des Petoudes) and soon emerge from the pinewoods in the little valley falling from the Glacier des Grands. Passing a few ruins the path now rises more steeply in zigzags, then slants to the right along a shelf tight against an impressive rock slab, the way safeguarded with fixed cable. Across this the path twists uphill again and a few moments later brings you to a group of converted alp buildings, one of which is the

REFUGE LES GRANDS (2113m, 2¼hrs) self-catering accommodation only, 15 dortoir places, cooking facilities, water supply, infrequently wardened, open mid-June to mid-Oct (for reservations Tel 026 660 65 04).

The continuing route to Col de Balme (**23**) leaves at the right-hand (north) end of the buildings, rising diagonally up the slope above the refuge to gain a high point at

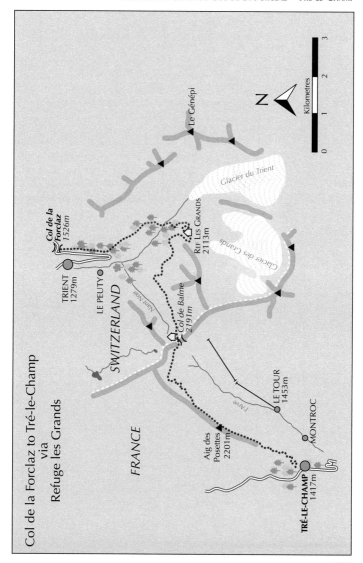

Col de la Forclaz to Tré-le-Champ
via
Refuge les Grands

about 2150m. The path twists among rocks, then eases as a very pleasant balcony among alpenrose and bilberry. While the view ahead is far-reaching and interesting, with the Dents du Midi providing focus, it's worth pausing to enjoy the backward view too. Here the little Glacier des Grands can be seen hanging in its cirque to the south, the larger Trient glacier beyond and to the left of that, while the route from the Fenêtre d'Arpette is easily detected across the valley.

As indicated at the head of this section, the path is an undulating one, and both the scenery and vegetation are delightful all the way. Several minor spurs are turned, which make you think the col is drawing near. Then, angling southwest, the mountainside becomes more stony and, in places, a little thin. Snow patches often lie across the path during the early weeks of the season, in which case caution needs to be exercised when crossing. But eventually the way rises a little, then eases down to a signed junction of paths a few paces from the

Views of Mont Blanc and the aiguilles are stunning from here.

REFUGE DU COL DE BALME (2191m, 3¾–4hrs) accommodation, refreshments; 26 dortoir places (Tel 04 50 54 02 33). ◀

The continuing route to **Tré-le-Champ** is described in Stage 9 (above).

STAGE 10
Tré-le-Champ – Refuge La Flégère

Start point	Tré-le-Champ (1417m)
Distance	8km (or 9km via Col des Montets *variante*)
Height gain	733m
Height loss	257m
Time	3½–4hrs (or 3½–3¾hrs by the *variante*)
High point	Tête aux Vents (2132m)
Transport option	Bus (Tré-le-Champ – Les Praz de Chamonix)
	Cablecar (Les Praz – La Flégère)
Accommodation	'Lac Blanc' – refuge
	La Flégère – privately-owned refuge
Alternative route	Tré-le-Champ – Col des Montets – La Flégère (see below)

The final two stages of the TMB adopt the highly acclaimed Grand Balcon Sud, one of the most scenic of all alpine belvedere paths, which runs along the mid-height slopes on the north side of the Vallée de l'Arve to provide an almost uninterrupted panorama of the Mont Blanc range. Pray that the weather will be kind enough to allow you to enjoy these stunning views, for they will ensure that your experience of the long circuit will end on a visual high note.

The altitude high point on this particular stage is a large cairn at a junction of paths. The cairn marks a boundary of the Réserve Naturelle des Aiguilles Rouges **(24)**. To reach it by the main route described below entails climbing a series of metal ladders, rungs, platforms and timber steps – the celebrated *passage délicat* – that some walkers may find troublesome, especially those with a tendency towards vertigo. From these artificial aids, which have been provided to overcome steep rock slabs, one gains a sensational bird's-eye view onto the rooftops of Argentière, 800m below.

There is, however, a way to avoid this section, a *variante* which begins further up the road from Tré-le-Champ towards the Col des Montets, and this is also described below (see box on page 118).

Another option (accessible from both the ladder route and the Col des Montets *variante*) goes to the famed Lac Blanc, a truly sensational vantage point whose refuge offers alternative overnight accommodation.

Should conditions be too bad to consider any of these options, and you've not enough time in hand to sit and wait a day or two in hope of an improvement, all is not lost. Either walk or take the bus downvalley to Les Praz de Chamonix, and ride the cablecar from there to La Flégère, spend a night in the refuge below the cablecar station, and hope for better weather next day in order to tackle the final stage to Les Houches.

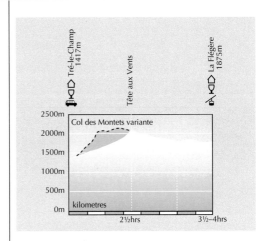

Out of Tré-le-Champ walk up the stony track to the main road, and cross with care to a footpath signed to Lac Blanc, La Flégère and Aiguillette d'Argentière. The way rises among trees and, passing a building, crosses the little Plan de la Grange. Heading southwest and rising all the time, mostly through open woodland, eventually come to a path junction where the left-hand option descends to Argentière. Bear right here and climb more steeply above the treeline towards a line of crags often used by activity centres and climbing schools. The most impressive rock feature is the monolithic Aiguillette d'Argentière, and the TMB path takes you right past its base (1893m).

It is here that you come to the first of the metal ladders and handrails that enable walkers to negotiate a

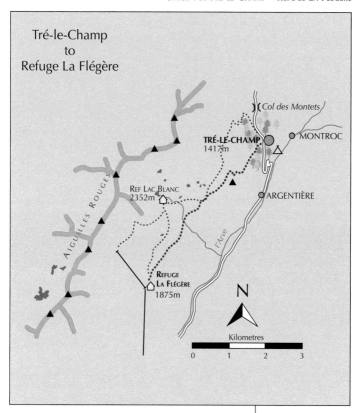

Tré-le-Champ
to
Refuge La Flégère

route up the steep rock walls. Although abruptly steep and seemingly endless, this whole series of aids should be perfectly safe – but beware of others climbing above you who may accidentally dislodge stones. Equally important, be careful not to dislodge anything onto anyone below.

At the top of the ladders the path rises again and suddenly comes to the large boundary cairn and path junction at the **Tête aux Vents** (2132m, 2hrs). The alternative route described in the box above is the path coming from the

TMB VARIANTE: TÊTE AUX VENTS VIA COL DES MONTETS

This route avoids the ladder section leading to the Tête aux Vents. It begins by going up to the main road above Tré-le-Champ, then walking up the road towards Col des Montets. After about 400m take a footpath on the left (1430m) signed Pédestre du Pays du Mont Blanc. Initially this takes you among plants with identification labels, then at a fork you take the left branch (to Lac Blanc and La Flégère), which soon angles north and meets another coming from Col des Montets. Turn left.

The gradient steepens and the path climbs in numerous zigzags to meet its demands, turning outcrops of rock and rising interminably, while views to the south show the first of the Chamonix aiguilles as a hint of even better things to come. At around 2000m the path eases onto a shoulder of hillside marked as La Remouaz on the map. This is where the Grand Balcon Sud officially begins. Now heading southwest the path forks again at 2060m, about 1hr 50mins after leaving Tré-le-Champ. Branch left on the Lac Blanc and Lac des Chéserys path and come to a large cairn at 2053m. Keep left at the next fork (the right branch veers off to the Lacs Chéserys and Blanc, the latter 1hr 20mins from here), and shortly after reach the prominent cairn of **Tête Aux Vents** (2132m, 2–2¼hrs) to join the main route.

One of the many entertaining ladder sections above Tré-le-Champ

right (sign for Col des Montets). The path ahead goes to Lac Blanc (see box below) and the Lacs des Chéserys, while we turn left for the Chalet des Chéserys and La Flégère.

LAC BLANC OPTION

Take the path ahead, signed to Lac de Chéserys and Lac Blanc. About 6mins later reach another path junction and turn left. Rising easily at first, the gradient steepens to pass above two of the Lacs de Chéserys, seen below to the right, then up again to cross a rocky knoll beyond which you come to the largest of the Chéserys lakes. Shortly after passing this lake, you come to another ladder-aided section, followed by a series of wood-braced steps before arriving at the privately-owned

REFUGE DU LAC BLANC (2352m, 3hrs) accommodation, refreshments; 40 dortoir places, manned from mid-June to end of Sept (Tel 04 50 53 49 14).

From Lac Blanc, and the tarn behind it, one of the finest of all Alpine views can be enjoyed, for your gaze is directed across the water to the distant Aiguilles Verte and Charmoz, with the glacial highway of the Mer de Glace between them, and the Grandes Jorasses dominating the backing wall; a simply magnificent view.

In order to reach Refuge La Flégère to rejoin the main TMB, cross the lake's outflow stream, pass the old refuge building and bear left. About 6mins below the lake the path forks and you take the left branch. Continuing down there are several other junctions, but at each the way is either clearly signed, or is obvious. Refuge La Flégère, below the cablecar station, is reached in about 1hr 10mins from Lac Blanc.

The panorama that bursts upon you at this cairn is just reward for the effort required to reach it. The whole north flank of the Mont Blanc range is spread out before you, an exquisite line of aiguilles, snow domes and glaciers. It's a view that gradually shuffles and rearranges the prominent players as the walk progresses, and nowhere along the Grand Balcon Sud does that panorama offer anything less than perfection. To quote Alexander Pope: 'And Alps upon Alps arise'.

Main TMB Route to La Flégère

Take the signed path for La Flégère and Chalet des Chéserys, both of which can be seen ahead. The way descends to another junction by the **Chalet des Chéserys** (2005m) in a further 10mins, and continues ahead ignoring alternatives to right and left. Wander across meadows towards a splendid waterfall spraying through a narrow gully in the cliff face on the right. The source of this is the idyllic Lac Blanc. Cross the stream flowing from it, and note that it then spills more cascades down the hillside below the path.

The way continues easily along the hillside with those panoramic views across the valley slowly developing new scenes as you progress. At the skiers' bar-restaurant La Chavanne (closed in summer) the immediate landscape is scarred by pistes, tracks and lifts, and the last few minutes of the walk are along one of these tracks, which takes you to **Refuge La Flégère** immediately below the cablecar station.

> **REFUGE LA FLÉGÈRE** (1875m, 3½–4hrs) accommodation, refreshments; 66 dortoir places, 21 beds; open mid-June to mid-Sept (Tel 06 03 58 28 14; bellay.catherine@wanadoo.fr).

Ignoring the ski-scarred landscape immediately behind the refuge, the view across the valley from the terrace is exquisite and of especial interest to TMB walkers, since it stretches from Col de Balme to Col de Voza. The Mer de Glace basin is directly opposite, flanked by the sharply defined Drus and snow-clad Verte on the left, the

Tiny Lac Flégère gives a mirror image similar to that from Lac Blanc

Aiguilles des Charmoz and Blaitière on the right. At the far end of the Mer de Glace **(25)** highway stands the solid wall of the Grandes Jorasses. To the right of the Blaitière are the Aiguilles du Plan and Midi, and then the summit of Mont Blanc itself, distinctly visible but perhaps less impressive than its neighbours from this angle, despite the lengthy Bossons glacier which tumbles from it. All in all, the scene is one of bewitching beauty. The refuge is comfortable, and when the cablecars cease for the day and evening settles over the mountains, the ambience is such to make a night spent here a truly memorable one.

LAC BLANC

After a reasonably short walk to get here it might be worth booking a bed and, leaving your rucksack behind, either walking up to Lac Blanc in about 1½hrs (a height gain of almost 480m) or taking the next stage of the chairlift beside the refuge up to l'Index, where an easy and very popular path contours along the hillside and leads directly to the lake. The refuge at the lake provides both refreshments and overnight accommodation (see box on page 119), and its situation is justifiably celebrated as having one of the great views of the Mont Blanc range, similar to that from La Flégère but from a loftier perspective and with the bonus of the view being reflected in the lake.

STAGE 11

Refuge La Flégère – Le Brévent –
Les Houches

Start point	Refuge La Flégère (1875m)
Distance	17km
Height gain	772m
Height loss	1546m
Time	6½hrs
High point	Le Brévent (2526m)
Accommodation	Bellachat (4–4½hrs) – privately-owned refuge
	Les Houches – hotels, dortoirs, gîte, camping
Transport options	Cablecar (La Flégère – Les Praz de Chamonix)
	Bus (Les Praz – Chamonix – Les Houches)
	Cablecar (Le Brévent – Chamonix)
	Train (Chamonix – Les Houches)

The final stage of the Tour of Mont Blanc is as varied as any on this walk. The scenic quality of the route remains unquestionably high, but at Plan Praz, on the way to Col du Brévent, the landscape has been reshaped and badly scarred on behalf of the downhill ski industry, with bulldozed pistes making a mockery of the Alpine environment that was for so long one of its primary appeals. But above this the col opens a window onto a different mountain world, before the TMB dips into a natural wilderness of boulder-choked hollows and limited views, relieved of its ruggedness only when the slope up to Le Brévent has been tackled.

Le Brévent was recognised in the 18th century as being an unrivalled viewpoint from which to study Mont Blanc in all its glory across the valley. The summit is crowned by a small café-snack bar, and a cablecar whisks visitors to within a few metres of the summit. But the visual splendour of that lofty panorama remains as magical as ever.

From here the seemingly never-ending descent to Les Houches is among the steepest and most tiring of the whole circuit, yet the perfect antidote to the walker's inevitable weariness is the constant step-by-step witness to Mont Blanc's unchallenged supremacy as the Monarch of the Alps. If that supremacy was ever in doubt, this final stage of the TMB will surely dispel any previously held scepticism.

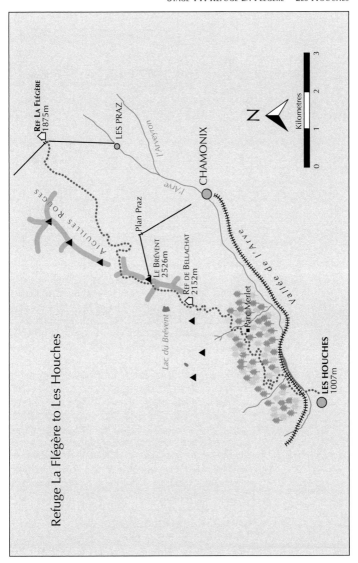

Refuge La Flégère to Les Houches

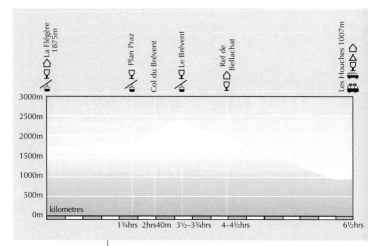

Surprising as it may seem, it will take almost 2hrs to reach Plan Praz from La Flégère, most of the way on a very pleasant path which begins by leaving the refuge terrace and cutting across the hillside just below the cablecar station. Shortly after this, fork right on a rising path which soon crosses a short rocky section eased with steps and a handrail. The TMB then makes a fine contour curving round successive hillside bays, one of which is open and rocky, but with masses of bilberries in late summer, before crossing a wooded spur into the open grasslands of **Charlanon** (1812m, 50mins). Crossing a track the path twists among shrubs and continues straight ahead at a cross-path, then beneath a chairlift and tight against cliffs followed by another contouring path leading to the track once more. Across this the TMB goes up a few steps and continues by making a traverse of the lower slopes of the Clocher de Planpraz before coming to a junction. Walk straight ahead on a broad stony track, rising in a curve across bare open slopes; the complex of lifts and pistes served by the Plan Praz cableway making this (along with the development around La Flégère) the most depressing sight of the whole TMB. But be patient, for once the climb

On the trail from La Flégère to Plan Praz

to Col du Brévent gets under way, the worst of it will be behind you.

After passing a junction where a path cuts off to Lac Cornu, keep ahead to the lift station of La Parsa at 2075m (Plan Praz is some way below). A sign here directs the TMB trail to the Col de Brévent – this is not the broad stony piste, but a good path which rises at an easy gradient before steepening towards the col. About 20–25mins up this path there's a junction at a bend (2197m). Be certain to turn sharp left here, for the alternative path approaches the Clocher de Plan Praz, which is well away from where we need to go.

Twisting its way upward with a direct view of the abrupt rocky face of Le Brévent, the path needs another 30mins to gain the **Col du Brévent** (2368m, 2hrs 40mins). It is on this saddle that the GR5 (La Grande Traversée des Alpes) **(26)** arrives from the Col d'Anterne, which can be seen to the northwest at the right-hand end of the great cliffs of the Rochers de Fiz. A brief rest is called for at the col in order to enjoy the contrasting views to north and south, because very shortly you will enter an enclosed hollow where your field of vision is severely restricted. Bouquetin (ibex) are known to inhabit this upper region, so keep alert for a possible sighting.

Now the TMB veers left and rises a little to enter a secluded basin where snow often lies in pockets well into the summer. In this wilderness of rocks and boulders the way is guided by an assortment of cairns and red spots, as well as the standard red–white waymark stripes. Climbing out of this hollow, two steel ladders and metal handrails aid the ascent of a steep section which might otherwise be a little tricky for those carrying a big rucksack. Then come onto a track/piste which rises up the northern slope of Le Brévent, with a view into the Diosaz valley and the distant Chaine des Aravis, on the way passing a small col on the left where a direct but less interesting route from Plan Praz emerges. Shortly after this reach another junction on a shoulder just below the Brévent summit. Although it's not essential to do so, if the weather is fine it would be difficult to resist the 5min diversion required to visit the top of this well-known mountain.

Le Brévent has long been famed for its direct view of Mont Blanc

Le Brévent (27) (2526m, 3½–3¾hrs, *refreshments*) provides an amazing full-frontal view of Mont Blanc, and an aerial perspective of Chamonix **(28)** lying almost 1500 vertical metres below – a sight almost as riveting as that of the glaciers opposite. In addition to the summit terrace

Refuge de Bellachat

with its modest café-bar, there's another restaurant at the head of the cableway just below the top.

Between the summit and the railway at Les Houches almost every step will now be downhill, a knee-wrenching, wearisome – but spectacular – descent, almost all the way on a good, if steep, path. From the junction just below the summit the TMB is signed to Bel Lachat. It descends in zigzags along little crests and into a rocky landscape which is left by a gap in its low enclosing ridge. There's nothing difficult about the route, and soon you can relax to enjoy the panorama, which should still have the power to excite as you wander down to grass slopes and, about 50mins or so from Le Brévent, come to a path junction on a grassy bluff. Just to the left, and tucked against the hillside, stands the

REFUGE DE BELLACHAT (2152m, 4–4½hrs) refreshments, accommodation, 28 dortoir places, open late-June to mid-Sept (Tel 04 50 53 43 23).

The outlook here is almost as magical as that from Le Brévent. Hogging the view is the long trunk of the Bossons glacier, which is seen full-length from top to bottom in all its rippled splendour across the way. Unless you have good reason to continue down to Les Houches or Chamonix, an overnight spent in this idyllic location is highly recommended.

Morning light throws shadows from the Chamonix aiguilles; the scene below Refuge de Bellachat

The path now descends to the right of the refuge, soon dropping in a series of zigzags down the precipitous flank of the Aiguillette de Brévent. The way descends into patches of forest and angles round to the right to the Vouillards ravine which has a stream running through it. This is gained by way of several metal steps with handrails for security. Across the stream the path soon takes you into forest again on the edge of the Parc Merlet mountain zoo (**29**). Waymarks around the zoo's perimeter fence indicate the route to the zoo's access road.

Follow this road to the right for a short distance away from the parking area, then take a path on the left which brings you quickly down to a good contouring section in woodland once more. Signs to follow at junctions are for Christ Roi and/or Les Houches, and about 20mins after leaving the zoo car park you arrive at the base of the towering concrete statue of Christ the King, or **Le Christ Roi** (**30**) (1196m, 6hrs).

A series of footpath shortcuts circumvents the track, which sweeps down to the valley in long loops, through forest almost all the way, until shortly before coming to the road that leads to the railway station below **Les Houches**, where the TMB began nearly two weeks and a host of memories ago. ◄

Now's the time to celebrate. You've earned it – congratulations!

PLACES AND ITEMS OF INTEREST ON THE TMB

The Bionnassay Glacier

1 Les Houches

Situated at the lowest and sunniest end of the Chamonix valley below the Aiguille du Goûter, the centre of Les Houches retains a pleasant village atmosphere, while the slopes above have been developed for skiing with access via several cableways. There are also some 30km of cross-country ski trails. During the summer, the bars, restaurants and campsite throng with TMB walkers, and it's not difficult to distinguish between those about to begin their tour and those who have just completed it. The staff at the tourist office in the main square are very helpful, and there's plenty of useful literature available.

2 The Mont Blanc Tramway

Claiming to be the highest rack-and-pinion railway in France, the tramway was built from 1907 to 1913 between Le Fayet (584m) below St-Gervais, and Nid d'Aigle overlooking the Bionnassay glacier at 2380m. Ambitiously planned to go right to the summit of Mont Blanc (until practicalities got in the way!), the journey rises through a series of tunnels and across viaducts to reach Col de Voza, then continues along the grassy spur of the Bellevue plateau (the tramway's upper limit in winter) before rising to its terminus at the 'Eagle's Nest' dominated by the Aiguille de Bionnassay. A path leads from the top station across the Désert de Pierre Rond, then descends to the moraine edge for close views of the Glacier de Bionnassay. Equally popular with sightseers and walkers, the tramway is often used by climbers setting out for an ascent of Mont Blanc by way of the Tête Rousse or Goûter refuges.

3 The Bionnassay Glacier

This tremendous glacier, contained between the Aiguilles du Goûter and Bionnassay, is one of the main background features on the route between Col de Voza and Les Contamines, being seen from a number of vantage points. In July 1892 the Tête Rousse feeder glacier broke up and collapsed causing a flood of water (the glacial torrent is said to have swollen to a depth of 25m) which swept through the Bionnassay valley, obliterating Bionnay and destroying much of St-Gervais-les-Bains. More than 200 lives were lost in the disaster.

4 Val Montjoie

The most westerly of the valleys that surround Mont Blanc, Val (or Vallée de) Montjoie measures a little over 20km from the Col du Bonhomme to Le Fayet, where the Bon Nant enters the Arve below St-Gervais-les-Bains. The valley has two notable gorges; one just behind Le Fayet, the other south of Les Contamines, a wooded cleft reaching from the pilgrim church at the roadhead to the Nant Borrant chalets. Elsewhere the valley is both open and sunny, and 2000 years ago the Roman legions

used it as a route of passage between the Val d'Aosta and Gaul, crossing passes traversed today by the Tour of Mont Blanc. Sections of paved Roman road can still be seen above Notre-Dame de la Gorge. In the 17th century some 2000 Waldensians came through the valley to escape the troops of Victor Amadeus II and, as the annals report, 'climbed one of the most difficult passes of the mountain known as the Bel-Homme amid snow and continuous rain ... where thirty men managed to halt an entire army.'

5 Les Contamines-Montjoie

An attractive resort with a handsome 18th-century church, Les Contamines makes a very fine base for a walking holiday with a number of excellent destinations, including Mont Joly, which stands across the valley and whose summit is noted for its view of the Mont Blanc range. According to Frison-Roche in *Mont Blanc and the Seven Valleys*, smuggling used to be predominant in the village right up to the early days of the 20th century.

6 Notre-Dame de la Gorge

This imposing Baroque chapel at the Val Montjoie roadhead is the scene of an annual pilgrimage that takes place on the Feast of the Assumption (15 August), and is approached past a series of roadside shrines. Inside, the building is replete with Renaissance frescoes and an ornate altar-piece.

Notre-Dame de la Gorge

of the Mont Blanc range, and was visited in 1781 by de Saussure and his guide, Pierre Balmat. An orientation table aids the identification of numerous features in the vast 360° panorama, which includes not only Mont Blanc, but the unmistakable stiletto point of the Matterhorn about 80km away.

9 Refuge de la Croix du Bonhomme

Standing a short distance below (and 40m lower than) the col after which it is named, the first hut to be built here was erected in the 1930s, destroyed during the war, and rebuilt in the 1960s (see the pictures in the hut book). That refuge was taken over and extended by the CAF in the 1990s – a curious mixture of architectural styles and materials, but a comfortable and welcoming hut for all that. Mont Pourri (3779m) is the

7 Réserve Naturelle des Contamines-Montjoie

This protected area extends over some 5500 hectares, effectively containing the upper reaches of the Val Montjoie and the eastern hillside above Les Contamines almost as far north as Le Champel, and reaching up to the ridge crest running from the Dômes de Miage to Col des Fours and across to the Aiguilles de la Pennaz. The *réserve* was created in 1979.

8 Tête Nord des Fours

Gained by an easy 15–20min walk from Col des Fours (crossed on a *variante* section of Stages 2 and 5) this minor 2756m summit is noted as a particularly fine viewpoint from which to study the southwestern side

Refuge de la Croix du Bonhomme

The Vallée des Glaciers with the Aiguille des Glaciers at its head

dominant peak visible from it, but it is the overall panorama, rather than any particular mountain, that provides the main scenic interest, especially during the evening, when the refuge is sometimes divorced from the valleys by skeins of mist. The refuge relies on solar panels for electricity, and hot water is only available for showers after 5pm – and then there's a rush!

10 Vallée des Glaciers

One of the smallest of Mont Blanc's seven valleys, it lies at the southwestern corner of the range, is sparsely inhabited and its only village (and that little more than a hamlet) is Les Chapieux, which is located some 18km from Bourg-St-Maurice. By tradition the various dairy farms of the valley were given over to the raising of Tarentaise cattle and the manufacture of Beaufort cheese. Despite impressions given by its name very few glaciers drain into the valley. In fact the name is taken from the Aiguille des Glaciers at its head, above Refuge des Mottets. The Aiguille, incidentally, is the southernmost of Mont Blanc's many attendant peaks. As for Les Chapieux, this is linked to busier, more inhabited valleys by way of the Route du Cormet de Roselend, which crosses the mountains between Bourg-St-Maurice and Albertville.

11 Col de la Seigne

Carrying the frontiers of France and Italy, the 2516m col has been breached, guarded, fought over and defended countless times since the Roman legions tramped across it, and customs posts on both flanks have only fallen into disuse since the 1980s. Of more interest to the TMB walker is the tremendous panoramic view which is one of the finest to be enjoyed by walkers anywhere in the Alps. In 1939 the alpine connoisseur RLG Irving wrote of it: 'The view of this side of the range is a fine contrast to that from the Col de Balme down the valley of Chamonix. In both cases Mont Blanc is the dominating personality; perhaps that is why the contrast is so marked, for we see here a very different Mont Blanc. At Chamonix it has the beauty of an aristocrat of the north, serene, majestic, a position assured by a long untroubled reign. Here it has a dark gypsy beauty, a wild disordered appearance that makes us feel that cataclysmic forces are still alive within it' (*The Alps*).

12 Val Veni

Also spelt Vény, this pastoral valley below the Lée Blanche provides a direct contrast to the soaring rock walls that guard it to the north. There are woods, meadows dotted with hay-barns, sidling streams and gravel beds, but the valley is almost cut off as an island by two big moraine walls that project into it and almost seclude it from the outside world. At its upper end, the Glacier de Miage and its moraine debris make a chaotic barrier, dividing the main valley from Lac Combal and the Vallon de la Lée Blanche. At the other end, opposite the start of Val Ferret across the mouth of Val d'Aosta, the moraine barrage of the Brenva glacier also threatens to close the Val Veni. In the early 1920s a huge mass of rock, estimated

Val Veni makes a deep trench below the south side of the Mont Blanc range

at around four million cubic metres, broke away from the Peuterey ridge and fell onto this glacier, sweeping away the seracs and spreading a chaos of rocks right across the valley, thus creating a dam blocking the river which led to the formation of a lake upvalley. Before further damage could be done, however, the water found escape underground and the lake disappeared. Then in January 1997 a similar collapse of rock and ice from Col Moore also fell on the Brenva glacier, blocking the valley again and destroying numerous trees.

13 Courmayeur

What Chamonix is to the French side of Mont Blanc, Courmayeur is to the Italian, except that Courmayeur has its own identity and an incomparably finer situation than its counterpart in France. Though set at a higher elevation than Chamonix, the climate here is warmer, the vegetation more varied. This, together with the discovery of mineral springs, gave early importance (albeit a rather low-key importance) to the village, which then attracted the aristocracy who built their villas and created parks in these sunny upper reaches of Val d'Aosta. Mont Blanc itself is hidden from view, but the huge south-facing walls of its satellite peaks are not. From the busy streets it looks like a gateway to the huge ramparts of the chain, guarded by Mont Chétif and Mont de la Saxe, and over it swings the cableway that links Courmayeur with Chamonix on a far more scenic journey than through the 16km-long Mont Blanc tunnel. Until

Courmayeur enjoys fine mountain views from every street

The Grand Col Ferret (2537m) on the borders of Italy and Switzerland is a grandstand from which to study the Italian Val Ferret

the tunnel was opened in the mid-1960s, Courmayeur enjoyed a sense of isolation and was far less commercially developed than Chamonix. The Mont Blanc tunnel was a mixed blessing: it lifted Courmayeur economically and brought the world to its streets.

14 The Italian Val Ferret

The 'official' route of the TMB no longer goes through the lower reaches of the Italian Val Ferret, preferring instead the beautiful north flank of Mont de la Saxe. Viewed from the Grand Col Ferret one sees in a glance that the two sides of the valley are totally different: the southern being refreshingly green and verdant,

the northern a rugged wall of rock cleft with ice. The same, in fact, as in the Val Veni. But by contrast with Val Veni, Ferret is not threatened by bulldozing glaciers and moraine earthworks. To be sure there are moraines in the valley bed but these have been largely disguised by vegetation. The lower valley, from Entrèves to La Vachey, is fairly narrow, but it begins to open out above La Vachey, and around Arnuva it's almost a plain, while the valley head at Pré de Bar (below the frontier ridge) has a showpiece glacier spilling down from Mont Dolent that attracts tourists using the summer bus service running through the valley between Courmayeur and Arnuva.

15 Rifugio Bonatti

Named after the great Italian mountaineer and adventurer Walter Bonatti, this large, comfortable and well-appointed hut stands on a pastoral hillside on the south side of the Val Ferret facing the Grandes Jorasses, and has a direct view from the dining room window of Mont Blanc in the west. Privately-owned and opened in August 1998, it's very much a model, both in design and facilities, for mountain huts of the present day. In keeping with its dedication, large photographs of or by Bonatti himself adorn the walls. Born in Bergamo in 1930, Walter Bonatti became a professional guide in 1954, and three years later settled in Courmayeur. His achievements in the Alps (most of which were in the Mont Blanc range, although he also made the first ascent – solo – of the Matterhorn's north face direct in 1965) put him among the ranks of the greatest of all climbers. In 1954 he was a member of the expedition that made the first ascent of K2 in the Karakoram, and four years later made the first ascent of Gasherbrum IV. After giving up top-grade climbing he turned to adventure travel, photography and journalism. His books include the autobiographical *On the Heights* (1964) and *The Great Days* (1974). Walter Bonatti died in Rome in 2011 aged 81.

16 Mont Dolent

This 3820m summit, where the frontiers of France, Italy and Switzerland meet, is the southeastern cornerstone of the Mont Blanc range. First climbed on 9 July 1864 by Whymper and Reilly with their guides, Michel Croz and Michel Payot, their route from Elena via the Petit Col Ferret is said to be straightforward and to present few difficulties. As for the summit, Whymper wrote that it was 'very small indeed; it was the loveliest

Rifugio Bonatti, on a hillside shelf above Val Ferret

little cone of snow that was ever piled up on mountain-top … it was a miniature Jungfrau, a toy summit, you could cover it with the hand.' If the summit is small, the view from it certainly is not. Adams-Reilly was emphatic: 'Situated at the junction of three mountain ridges, it rises in a positive steeple far above anything in its immediate neighbourhood; and certain gaps in the surrounding ridges … extend the view in almost every direction … [the view is] as extensive, and far more lovely than that from Mont Blanc itself.'

17 La Fouly

Despite its modest size, this small village deep inside the Swiss Val Ferret is *the* centre for climbing and walking above all others in the valley, and it was a great favourite with such writers as Emile Javelle and Charles Gos. It can seem overpoweringly gloomy in bad weather, but when the sun shines it positively glows. La Fouly faces across the Drance de Ferret into the glorious cirque of La Neuvaz overhung by the elegant Tour Noir (3836m), which is counter-balanced by Mont Dolent.

18 Champex

Tranquil is the word best used to describe this trim Swiss resort, set beside a small lake on a natural shelf between Val d'Arpette and Val Ferret. One or two fanciful hotels in the style of the Belle Epoque look across the water to the Grand Combin;

anglers either line the banks in the early morning or sit patiently in their boats transmitting the calm that is the essence of the place. Despite its proximity to outliers of the Mont Blanc range, and despite the fact that it first came to the attention of visitors in the late 19th century as a mountaineering centre, Champex seems strangely divorced from vertical adventures.

Rather than a centre for activity, these days it suggests rest and relaxation. The TMB walker needs to soak up that atmosphere for just one night then move on, lest he become seduced into remaining behind to lie in the sun and dream. For anyone choosing to take a rest-day here, the La Breya cableway offers a means of gaining a fine viewpoint, with prospects of a short walk to the Cabane d'Orny. Alternatively one could visit the local alpine garden (Flore Alpe) on the hillside north of the village, which contains more than 4000 plants and is reckoned to be the finest collection in Switzerland (open May to Sept; Tel 027 783 12 17; www.flore-alpe.ch).

19 Col de la Forclaz

This 1526m pass provides the shortest road route between Martigny and Chamonix, and is thus a crossing of some importance. The road took from 1825 to 1887 to build, but the first motor vehicle did not cross until 1912. In those days traffic was forbidden to travel at night, and the speed limit was 18kph. Before the road reached Forclaz travellers had to negotiate no less than 36 hairpin bends on the way from Martigny. Whymper crossed in July 1864, complaining that the east side of the col was 'not creditable to Switzerland. The path from Martigny to the summit has undergone successive improvements,' he reported, 'but mendicants permanently disfigure it. We passed many tired pedestrians toiling up this oven, persecuted by trains of parasitic children. These children swarm there like maggots in a rotten cheese. They carry baskets of fruit with which to plague the weary tourist. They flit around him like flies; they thrust the fruit in his face; they pester him with their pertinacity. Beware of them!' Be assured they are not there now, but the fruit is excellent.

20 Val d'Arpette

Sometimes referred to as Arpettaz, this charming little valley above Champex is a barely inhabited gem of unspoilt nature. With a forest of spruce and fir in its lower reaches, meadows full of alpine flowers in the spring and a clear mountain torrent winding through its middle regions, it's closed off in the west by craggy converging ridges that send down huge slopes of scree and boulders, and shine with the last remnants of the little Ecandies glacier below the Pointe d'Orny. As Frison-Roche put it: 'This is scenery straight from a geography atlas, showing in one picture the habitat, the fauna, the flora and the mountain-formation… The Val d'Arpettaz is so satisfying; there you can still breathe the gentle air of solitude' (*Mont Blanc and the Seven Valleys*).

View of Trient

21 Vallée du Trient

The valley proper starts at the foot of the retreating Glacier du Trient and stretches for less than 8km to the Tête Noir gorges where the torrent, fed by the snow lake of the Plateau du Trient, pours into the Eau Noire. This isolated upper valley, settled only at Le Peuty and Trient (Le Gilliod), is an obvious glacial trough. Long ago a small glacier lay below the Col de Balme and was responsible for scooping out the hanging valley used by the TMB. This has completely disappeared, leaving only the Glacier des Grands, in a cirque above Refuge Les Grands, and the main Glacier du Trient at the head of the valley as witnesses to the past.

22 Bisse du Trient

Flowing from the torrent below the Glacier du Trient to Col de la Forclaz, this is just one of more than 200 such irrigation channels created in the Swiss Valais. Of great importance in dry weather to the agricultural economy of the Rhône valley, these *bisses* were used to carry glacial water to cultivated fields far below. The oldest date back to the 12th and 13th centuries; in places they were hacked out of bare rock, in others hollow tree trunks were used to bridge areas impossible to excavate. Many were made by prisoners used as forced labour. Footpaths invariably ran alongside the *bisses* to aid their maintenance, and in the late 19th century the Bisse du Trient had rails laid alongside it on which ice blocks were transported to the hotel at the Col de la Forclaz.

23 Col de Balme

Overlooking the Vallée de l'Arve from the frontiers of France and Switzerland, this easy 2191m pass makes a tremendous viewpoint. The valley of Chamonix projects ahead and far below, flanked on the left by the Aiguilles du Tour, d'Argentière, Verte and Drus, the ragged aiguilles of Charmoz and Blaitière clustered together, and then the majestic snowy crown of Mont Blanc beyond and above everything. As RLG Irving once wrote (in *The Alps*), 'If that view does not thrill you you are better away from the Alps.' In an earlier age Baedeker called it 'a superb view', while Frison-Roche, who knew the range better than most, described the arrival at the col: 'You reach it gradually without getting any inkling of the secrets on the other side. Then, all of a sudden, there is the upthrust of countless peaks soaring into the sky and the whole of the Chamonix valley appears, wide and gently curving, fading into the blue haze and purple tints of the far-away Prarion.'

24 Réserve Naturelle des Aiguilles Rouges

Founded in 1974, and situated between Argentière and Vallorcine, the Aiguilles Rouges nature reserve seeks to protect a series of high Alpine habitats on the north flank of the Vallée de l'Arve, a boundary of which runs along the summit ridge of the aiguilles themselves. The diverse habitats of the area account for 594 different species of plants, 84 birds and 23 mammals including, of course, marmot, chamois and bouquetin (ibex). The Chalet d'accueil (Information Centre) on the Col des Montets houses a variety of displays and items of literature, and shows videos and slide presentations about the reserve.

25 Mer de Glace

The longest, widest and highest of Mont Blanc's many glaciers, the Mer de Glace is, after the Grosser Aletschgletscher in the Bernese Alps, the second longest of all those in the Alpine chain, and is fed by no less than 14 other icefields. Ever since the visit by William Windham and Richard Pococke in 1741, it has been a focus for the admiring attention of tens of thousands of non-mountaineering visitors to Chamonix. Formerly these visitors would have been carried to the Montenvers Hotel by mule, but in 1908 a steam-driven rack railway operated between Chamonix and the hotel viewpoint, and this was modernised in 1993. A popular early excursion was the crossing of the glacier to Le Chapeau, a rock projection above the right-hand lateral moraine. To cross the glacier travellers were advised to wear 'woollen socks to draw over shoes unfurnished with nails'. Thanks to glacial recession Le Chapeau is now a long way from the snout of the Mer de Glace, helped no doubt by the collapse of the glacial tongue in 1922 which caused serious flooding in Chamonix, when

blocks of ice were deposited in the Place de Saussure. Today the Mer de Glace is regularly used as a highway of approach to the heartland of the massif and the many huts from which climbs are made.

26 GR5 – La Grande Traversée des Alpes

This epic route, which stretches for some 660km from Lac Léman (the Lake of Geneva) to Nice on the Mediterranean coast, covers the most dramatic and scenically enriching section of the much longer European trail, the E2, which begins at Ostend in Belgium. Making a full traverse of the French Alps, it shares the route of the TMB from Col du Brévent to Col de la Croix du Bonhomme. A guidebook to this challenging trek is published by Cicerone Press, *The GR5 Trail* by Paddy Dillon.

27 Le Brévent

This celebrated 2526m viewpoint is thought to have had its first ascent by a tourist in 1760, when it was climbed by the 20-year-old Horace Bénédict de Saussure with his guide, Pierre Simon. Of course the whole of this upper ridge system on the north side of the Vallée de l'Arve would by then have been frequented by chamois hunters and even shepherds, but it was de Saussure who put the summit on the map as one of the finest of elevated points, if not *the* finest, from which to study Mont Blanc. Saussure, and others after him, came there to

Le Brévent, the summit café/bar with its view of Mont Blanc

prospect a route to the summit of the then unclimbed Mont Blanc, and after it had been climbed locals would go up onto the Brévent to see for themselves the victorious mountaineers (albeit tiny specks of mountaineers) on that snowy crown across the valley. The Brévent *téléphérique* from Chamonix was erected between 1928 and 1930, thus enabling all and sundry who could afford a ticket to enjoy one of the great panoramas of the Alps.

28 Chamonix

With Mont Blanc as a backdrop, Chamonix is the world's greatest mountaineering centre. The site of a Benedictine priory founded in the 11th century, the small commune of farmers and hunters adopted the name by which it is known today as early as 1330, but it was not until the 18th century that Chamonix bought its freedom from the sometimes harsh priory rule, and became known to a wider public thanks to the visit of Pococke and Windham in 1741. Thereafter the 'Vale of Chamouni' was established as the cradle of mountain devotion and a focus of attention for all would-be mountaineers. Being clearly seen from far-away Geneva, and recognised as the highest in the Alps, Mont Blanc naturally attracted the studious and the curious, the athletic and the adventurous. Gathered at its feet, Chamonix learned to live off the mountain and came to prosper by it. By 1800 it had

The ever-busy Avenue Michel Croz in Chamonix

become the first real tourist centre in the Alps. The sport of mountaineering was virtually conceived here, and the reputation gained in the 18th century has not wavered in more than 200 years, during which time the town's appeal has broadened to encompass every aspect of mountain activity as well as general tourism. The first ever Winter Olympics were held here in 1924, and skiing now rivals climbing and walking as the town's number one sport. Although crowded in summer and winter alike, the assortment of mechanised lift systems manages to distribute visitors over a wide area. Among these the Aiguille du Midi cablecar, which carries passengers to 3842m, is the most spectacular, for

it links with a gondola system that continues across the Vallée Blanche to Pointe Helbronner, where another cableway descends to Entrèves, near Courmayeur, on the Italian side of the range. There's also the Mer de Glace railway and assorted cableways leading onto the slopes of the Aiguilles Rouges on the valley's north side. From them there's a veritable wonderland of footpaths to explore. (Chamonix tourist information can be found on the Place du Triangle de l'Amitié Tel 04 50 53 00 24, www.chamonix.com.)

29 Parc Merlet Mountain Zoo

Properly known as the Parc du Balcon de Merlet, this 20 hectare site is located on a promontory of forest and pasture on the lower slopes of the Aiguillet du Brévent opposite Taconnaz. The zoo contains typical mountain animals, both Alpine and exotic species, and includes chamois, bouquetin, marmot, llama and moufflon. Occupying a prime site with direct views to Mont Blanc, Parc Merlet is open to the public from May to Sept, 10.00–18.00; July and August 9.00–19.30 (Tel 04 50 53 47 89).

30 Le Christ-Roi

This 17m-high statue of Christ the King, which stands on the edge of forest opposite Les Houches and is floodlit at night, was made of reinforced concrete in the 1930s by sculptor M Serraz, and was paid for by donations from holidaymakers and local residents.

THE STORY OF MONT BLANC

Although the Tour of Mont Blanc neither ventures onto a glacier nor makes any pretence at climbing in any technical sense, the mountain range that forms the central theme of the route has been at the forefront of mountaineering activity for more than 200 years. It was during the 18th and early 19th centuries that the 'Vale of Chamouni' was visited by educated young men as part of the European Grand Tour. Many would go as far as the source of the Arveyron and Montenvers, but the more daring crossed a glacier or two in the care of local men who, having come to know the mountains from their work as chamois or crystal hunters, set themselves up as guides.

Living within sight of Mont Blanc a wealthy Genevese scientist, Horace Bénédict de Saussure, became fascinated by that distant vision, and in 1760 went alone to see the glaciers close at hand. Excited by what he found, he offered a substantial reward to whoever could discover a route to Mont Blanc's summit. Although the prize sparked little immediate response, it became the catalyst not only for the ascent of the highest mountain in the Alps, but for the sport of mountaineering as we know it today.

The west face of Mont Blanc

It was 15 years before any serious attempt was made. On 12 July 1775 four local men spent the night on the slopes of the Montagne de la Côte above Les Bossons, and next day worked their way up the spur to the Grand Mulets, but failed to make much progress beyond it. Two months later Thomas Blaikie, a Scottish botanist, arrived on the scene and, in the company of 18-year-old Michel-Gabriel Paccard, youngest son of the Chamonix notary, embarked on the first serious exploration of the range. In the course of a week's travel they climbed the Brévent, traversed below the Chamonix aiguilles, crossed the Bossons glacier to the head of the Montagne de la Côte, climbed the Taconnaz glacier and approached the Aiguille du Goûter, then went up the Mer de Glace to the Jardin de Talèfre. Although this adventuring was primarily in search of plants, it no doubt inspired Paccard's own interest in climbing Mont Blanc himself.

In 1783 Paccard, by now the Chamonix doctor, made his first attempt on the mountain with Marc-Théodor Bourrit, the pompous and egocentric Precentor of Geneva Cathedral. Choosing an identical route of approach as that of the 1775 attempt, they were no more successful than their predecessors, giving up before entering the icy valley formed by the Taconnaz and Bossons glaciers which rises directly to the summit. Bourrit, it appears, was afraid to set foot on the ice, yet despite his timidity he began a campaign to

stir up public interest in Mont Blanc's ascent with a view to publishing a best-selling account of the climb.

The following year Dr Paccard and his assistant Pierre Balmat explored the glacial basin above Montenvers, and three months later studied the northwest flank of the mountain above Bionnassay. Crossing the Cols de Voza and Tricot, they then climbed the slopes of the Aiguille de Goûter to a point high above the Tête Rousse. When Bourrit got to hear of it he took five guides with him and tried to advance Paccard's route. Again his courage failed and he went no further than the Tête Rousse, but two of his guides continued to the Dôme du Goûter and on to the band of rocks on which the Vallot hut now stands. Ahead rose the snow humps of the Bosses ridge, which must have seemed formidable for, little more than 300m from Mont Blanc's summit, the guides turned back.

In June 1786 two separate parties set out to compare the Dôme du Goûter route with the original Montagne de la Côte option. The Montagne de la Côte men arrived at the Col du Dôme an hour and a half before the others, and when the two parties were at last united they built a cairn on the Vallot rocks before descending together, leaving behind a young crystal hunter, Jacques Balmat, who wanted more time to search the Rochers Foudroyés. Caught out by nightfall, Balmat was forced to spend the night on the glacier, proving to

Looking towards the Grandes Jorasses in the Mont Blanc range

everyone's surprise that it was possible to survive a bivouac at such altitudes.

For three years Paccard had been studying Mont Blanc, accumulating experience of the mountain and concluding that the Bosses ridge was impractical. Having spent hours scanning every detail through a telescope he concluded that his only chance of success was to tackle the mountain face-on. Anxious to try this route he accepted Balmat's offer to take the place of his preferred guide who was away at the time, and engaged the crystal hunter as porter to carry the provisions, a blanket, barometer and tripod.

On 7 August 1786 the two men bivouacked near the top of the Montagne de la Côte, and at 4.00am next morning began their ascent. Having no rope they relied on their iron-pointed batons as the sole means of support in negotiating a maze of crevasses. Route-finding was difficult, the snow was soft and it took eight hours to get past the Grands Mulets. By mid-afternoon they had gained the Grand Plateau, a vast desert of snow and ice between the Dôme du Goûter and Mont Maudit. Balmat became disillusioned and wanted to give up, saying that he was needed at home where his child was dying. But Paccard persuaded him to continue, shouldered some of the load and helped force the route.

Above the Grand Plateau the angle steepened, the temperature dropped and it seemed likely that

145

In the centre of Chamonix, a statue shows Balmat pointing out the route to Mont Blanc's summit to de Saussure

the doctor and the crystal hunter reached the summit together, tied a kerchief to a baton and planted it in the snow as a victory flag. Chamonix was watching, and two men hurried to Geneva to report the news to de Saussure.

Sadly the first ascent of Mont Blanc quickly turned to controversy fuelled by the jealousy of Marc-Théodor Bourrit and the embellished account of the climb given by Balmat, which raised his status to that of local celebrity and international hero and denegrated Paccard, who was largely ignored. Balmat was honoured by the King of Savoy and Sardinia, and later immortalised by the raising of a statue in Chamonix which shows him pointing out the route to de Saussure. Saussure, however, left behind an assessment of Paccard's character which can be used as a true reference: 'This modest and sympathetic character has been ... unjustly relegated to the second rank behind the somewhat theatrical figure of his countryman... Paccard was a mountaineer of great merit.' A bust in his memory was finally unveiled in Chamonix in 1932.

they would have to endure a high bivouac. Yet however much they may have dreaded the prospect, they knew now that survival was possible and found the courage to continue. Once they'd overcome the Rochers Rouges the summit was in sight and they smelt success at last. At 6.23pm

THE TOUR OF MONT BLANC
CLOCKWISE

Aiguille Verte towers over Les Drus in this telephoto shot from Col de Balme

STAGE 1
Champex – Ferret

Start point	Champex (1466m)
Distance	18km
Height loss	420m
Height gain	650m
Time	5hrs
Low point	Issert (1055m)
Transport options	Postbus (Champex – Orsières)
	Postbus (Orsières – La Fouly – Ferret)
Accommodation	Champex – hotels, pensions, gîte, camping
	La Fouly (4hrs) – hotels, gîte, camping
	La Léchère (4¾hrs) – gîte
	Ferret – hotel

This first stage of the circuit is an easy valley walk along the eastern edge of the Mont Blanc range, giving an opportunity to develop a pace and stride that will carry you comfortably throughout the tour. The snow-capped Combin massif is on show at the start, but once you've descended to the bed of Val Ferret, this disappears and it will take a while before big mountains are once more on display. But at La Fouly a tremendous amphitheatre is revealed as a foretaste of the many good things to come during the days ahead.

Although high mountains are not a major feature on this section of the tour, the walk is by no means uninteresting. In fact Val Ferret is a charming pastoral valley whose old timber chalets and haybarns recall a long-lost era, for the farming communities based around a string of small villages and hamlets appear to have resisted the advent of our technological age, and one wanders among scenes of peaceful antiquity.

CHAMPEX (18) (1466m) Tourist information (Tel 027 775 23 83; champexlac@saint-bernard. ch; **www.champexinfo**); hotels, pension, gîte, camping; restaurants, shops, PTT. Lower-priced accommodation: Pension En Plein

Champex-Lac, a restful site surrounded by mountains

Air, 48 dortoir places, 25 beds, open all year (Tel 027 783 23 50, pensionenpleinair@bluewin.ch); Au Club Alpin, 25 dortoir places, open all year (Tel 027 783 11 61); Chalet du Jardin Alpin, 8 dortoir places, 13 beds, self-catering only, open May to end Oct (Tel 027 783 12 17; info@flore-alphe.ch); Camping Les

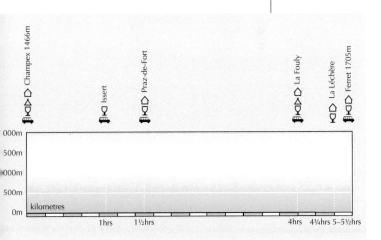

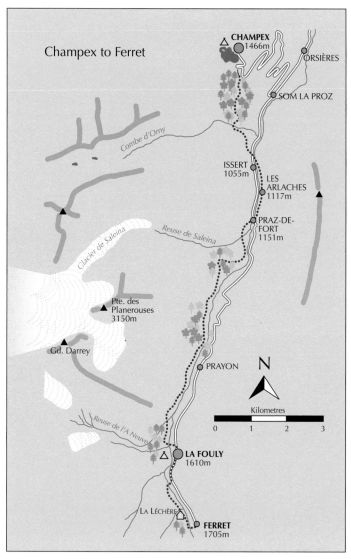

Champex to Ferret

△ **CHAMPEX**
1466m

● ORSIÈRES

● SOM LA PROZ

Combe d'Orny

ISSERT
1055m

LES
ARLACHES
1117m

PRAZ-DE-
FORT
1151m

Reuse de Saleina

Glacier de Saleina

▲ Pte. des
Planerouses
3150m

▲ Gd. Darrey

● PRAYON

N

Kilometres

0   1   2   3

Reuse de l'A Neuve

△ **LA FOULY**
1610m

LA LÉCHÈRE △ ● **FERRET**
1705m

Rocailles, open all year (Tel 027 783 19 79) is located at the top end of the village.

At the southeastern end of the lake, take a minor road on the left signed to the Fort d'artillerie. After about 200m cross an open area on the right to join a service road near Hotel Bellevue. Turn right and soon come onto a track, then footpath, that winds above the main Champex to Orsières road, keeping mostly among trees. The path eventually brings you onto the road near a left-hand bend. Cross with care to the signed TMB which is shared by the Sentier des Champignons. For much of the descent through woodland the trail is decorated with wood carvings depicting mushrooms, squirrels, an eagle and so on.

The way now takes an undulating course through forest, and when alternatives are offered the TMB route is either waymarked with a yellow diamond outlined in black or is clearly obvious. About 40mins from the start the path makes a deep indent to a stream, which it crosses by footbridge, and shortly after this comes onto a track at a hairpin bend. Walk down the track, and when it makes another hairpin a signed footpath descends steeply at first then, emerging from the woods, eases along the hillside

Praz-de-Fort and the pastoral Swiss Val Ferret

with a view into the Val Ferret ahead. Once again come onto a track, cross a stream, then walk down to the main road about 100m south of Issert.

Issert (1055m, 55–60mins, *refreshments*) is a small village astride the road, with a café which may be of interest if you're in need of refreshment. Halfway through the village turn left between buildings, cross the Drance de Ferret river and follow the narrow road/track which swings to the right and heads upvalley among meadows. At a T-junction of tracks turn left, rising at first then curving to the right. At the next junction continue ahead, and as you approach the hamlet of Les Arlaches outliers of the Mont Blanc range are seen rising along the valley's right-hand wall.

Les Arlaches (1117m, 1hr 15mins) has neither accommodation nor refreshment facilities, but it does have some attractive corners where old barns and chalets crowd together. Walk right through the hamlet and on between more meadows to

PRAZ-DE-FORT (1151m, 1½hrs) refreshments, PTT, grocery.

On entering the village turn right on the main road, cross the river and take the second turning on the left (sign to Cabane de Saleinaz), and follow TMB waymarks up through the village streets, and out to cross the mouth of Val de Saleina.

The tarmac lane becomes a dirt road, and when you see a bridge on the left, take a footpath on the right which climbs into forest. Initially a steady climb, the way then eases along a natural causeway between trees. This causeway is in fact an old moraine, the so-called Crête de Saleina, bulldozed long ago by the retreating Glacier de Saleina. The 'causeway' ends at a path junction where the TMB turns sharp left. When the path forks moments later take the upper option. This now gains height along the steep wooded hillside, and before long climbs in zig-zags to a slightly exposed open section safeguarded by a length of fixed chain. Beyond this the way rises a little further, then begins a steady descent.

On coming to a track at a hairpin bend, walk ahead. The track forks by a bridge, but the TMB maintains direction, keeping to the right of the river and rising again at a steady gradient. About 9mins beyond the fork a side route cuts left to Prayon.

Ignoring this alternative keep ahead. The way eventually becomes a footpath through a mixture of forest and meadow before reverting to track again. When it forks, with one branch breaking sharply to the right, continue straight ahead into forest, eventually coming onto a metalled service road. Bear left along this, and about 120m later turn left to cross the river by a sluice. Over this go up a slope among larch trees, then turn right opposite Grand Hotel du Val Ferret and walk into **La Fouly (17)**. From the main street there are splendid views across the valley into a cirque of mountains crowned by Mont Dolent **(16)** and the Tour Noir.

LA FOULY (1610m, 4hrs) hotels, gîte, camping, supermarket, restaurants, PTT, ATM, tourist information (Tel 027 775 23 84; **www.lafouly.ch/en**). Lower-priced accommodation: Chalet Le Dolent, 65 dortoir places,

Above La Fouly bristling ridges and small glaciers contrast with the valley meadows

10 beds, open all year (Tel 027 783 29 31; info@
dolent.ch; **www.dolent.ch**); Gîte Les Girolles, 60
beds, open all year (Tel 027 783 18 75; lesgirolles@
netplus.ch); Auberge des Glaciers, 34 dortoir places,
22 beds, open June to October (Tel 027 783 11 71;
info@aubergedesglaciers.ch); Hotel Edelweiss, 25
dortoir places, 45 beds, open end of May to end of Sept
(Tel 027 783 26 21; hotel.edelweiss@st-bernard.ch).

Walk through the village along the main road, and 8mins
later descend to the river on a track/dirt road. Across
the river bear left on a footpath which angles uphill
among trees and emerges to an open meadow, at the
top of which you come onto a crossing track and turn
left. Edging round the hillside above the west bank of the
river, the track soon looks ahead to the valley's last settle-
ment, the small village of Ferret. On coming to a broad
path climbing on the right, note that this leads to the

GÎTE DE LA LÉCHÈRE (4¾hrs) accommodation,
refreshments; 35 dortoir places, open June to end Sept
(Tel 079 433 49 78; **www.lalechere.ch**).

Unless you plan to spend the night, or need refreshments
there, remain on the track, but shortly after take a path
cutting across the hillside on the right, with a second spur
climbing from it to the gîte. Cross a bridge spanning a
side stream and wander ahead through lovely riverside
woodland to a footbridge across the Drance de Ferret.
Over the bridge walk up the slope to

FERRET (1705m, 5–5½hrs) accommodation,
refreshments. Hotel Col de Fenêtre, 18 dortoir places,
17 beds, open June to end Sept (Tel 027 783 11 88;
bertrandmurisier@bluewin.ch).

STAGE 2
Ferret – Grand Col Ferret – Rifugio Bonatti

Start point	Ferret (1705m)
Distance	17km
Height gain	1260m
Height loss	825m
Time	5½–6hrs
High point	Grand Col Ferret (2537m)
Transport option	Bus (Arnuva – La Vachey – Courmayeur)
Accommodation	La Peule (1hr 10mins) – refuge
	Pré de Bar (3¼–3½hrs) – refuge
	Arnuva (4–4¼hrs) – gîte
	Rifugio Bonatti – privately-owned refuge

After just one day's walking in Switzerland the TMB crosses into Italy, exchanging one Val Ferret for another. The crossing is not a difficult one under normal summer conditions, for the Grand Col Ferret lies at the head of modestly angled grass slopes, and the path to it is, for the most part, well defined. The col makes a wonderful viewpoint. From it you scan the full length of the Italian side of the Mont Blanc range, with Val Ferret running into Val Veni, while the Col de la Seigne (which takes the route out of Italy and into France in three days' time) should be clearly visible at the far end.

Initially there are two options to begin the approach to the Grand Col Ferret; one a high route, the other an easy valley walk, but the two unite at the small dairy farm of La Peule. Above this alp, the bold profile of the Grandes Jorasses rises over a beckoning ridge, and once the col has been topped, many other fine mountains and hanging glaciers are revealed. This first pass of the route proves to be a truly memorable one.

Descent to the Italian Val Ferret is straightforward, with the path leading directly to Rifugio Elena, a modern hotel-like hut perfectly situated at the head of the valley and providing temptations for refreshment in full view of the Pré de Bar glacier. Then comes a brief valley walk before climbing onto a delightful balcony path that leads to Rifugio Bonatti, another well-appointed hut on a natural terrace directly opposite the Grandes Jorasses, and with a view downvalley to Mont Blanc itself.

TMB VARIANTE

Leaving Ferret walk upvalley along the road for about 20mins, where you reach the official roadhead just below the dairy farm of Les Ars dessous. A small buvette (*refreshments*) stands a few metres up the track to the left. Descend a dirt road to a bridge spanning the Drance de Ferret at 1770m. The view downstream from here shows a crusty ridge of peaks and their hanging glaciers that carry the Franco-Swiss border. Cross the bridge and follow the farm road that winds steadily uphill to reach another dairy farm,

ALPAGE LA PEULE (2071m, 1hr 10mins) accommodation, refreshments; 30 places; open in summer (Tel 027 783 10 44; coppey.lapeule@dransnet. ch; www.lapeulaz.skyrock.com).

Walk alongside the long alp building until you rejoin the main TMB route.

Main TMB Route
From Ferret descend to the river, cross the footbridge to a path junction and walk straight ahead up the steep slope to a second signed junction. Continue uphill among larches, then over an open slope on the eastern side of the combe of Les Creuses to reach a small concrete hut. The trail now swings left, and shortly after you turn a spur out of the combe and follow an

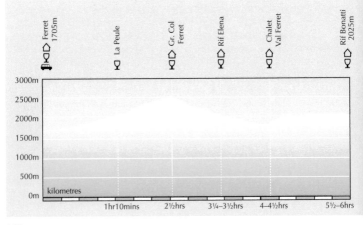

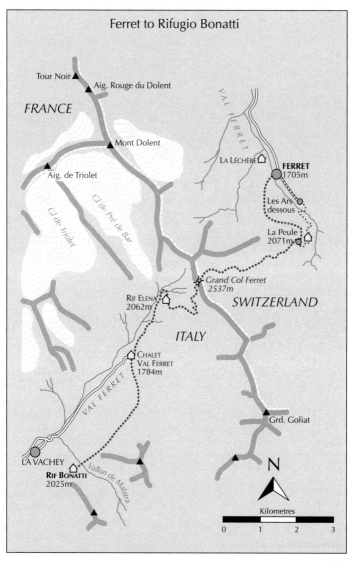

Ferret to Rifugio Bonatti

Early light on the Tour Noire, as seen from Ferret

undulating course along the steep vegetated hillside. The way cuts into minor grooves and gullies before contouring across an open pasture to reach the uppermost buildings of

LA PEULE (2071m, accommodation in dorms and yurts, refreshments – details in 'TMB Variante' above) about 1½hrs from Ferret. Here you join the alternative route and rise again above the dairy farm.

After gaining about 150m or so the gradient eases, and the path cuts round the hillside in a gently rising traverse above the combe of Revers de la Peule, where the top of the Grandes Jorasses comes into view to the west. With a few undemanding stretches you enter a vast upland basin with the signpost marking the Grand Col Ferret clearly visible. A little over an hour from La Peule, at an altitude of about 2400m, a minor path breaks away from the main trail, cutting sharply to the right. A short 2min diversion along this will bring you to a surprise view down the length of the Val Ferret.

The Italian Val Ferret

Regain the original path and continue to the col in another 10–15mins. Snow often lies on the Swiss side of the pass until the middle of summer, but the route should be clear, with marker poles sometimes leading the way.

Grand Col Ferret (2537m, 2½–2¾hrs) is both a watershed and an international boundary. Streams flowing down the Italian slope feed into the Po and eventually into the Adriatic, while rain falling on the Swiss side works its way via the Rhône to the Mediterranean. An orientation table on the saddle helps identify many peaks that bring character to the panorama, as well as mentioning some that no naked eye could see – the Matterhorn, for example. But the most outstanding feature of the view is the deep cut of the Italian Vals Ferret **(14)** and Veni, with the Grandes Jorasses and Mont Dolent **(16)** claiming the mountain honours nearby. Behind to the east the Grand Combin and Mont Vélan are appealing.

The path down to Rifugio Elena has been unravelled into several braidings, all obvious but fairly steep for much of the way, and the *rifugio* is in sight long before you reach it. Views are excellent throughout the

45–50min descent. The hut has been built on the rumpled Pré de Bar pasture at the very head of the valley, a long glacial tongue directly opposite being squeezed down the mountainside from a *firn* basin rimmed by Mont Dolent and Aiguille de Triolet. On the descent from the col the full length of this glacier is on show.

> **RIFUGIO ELENA** (2062m, 3¼–3½hrs) accommodation, refreshments; 128 dortoir places, 15 beds; manned mid-June to mid-Sept (Tel 01 65 84 46 88; rifugioelna@virgilio.it).

Below Rifugio Elena, the trail provides a view of the Triolet glacier to the left of the Monts Rouges de Triolet

The TMB path descends to the roadhead at Arnuva by following a waymarked path behind Rifugio Elena. The unmade service road linking the hut with Arnuva could also be taken, but this is often very busy with day visitors who come to gaze at the Pré de Bar glacier and take refreshment at the hut. Whichever route is taken, in about 40mins you come to a large parking area where the footpath route descends onto the track. After crossing a bridge over the river, immediately turn left to

CHALET VAL FERRET (1784m, 4–4¼hrs) bar/
restaurant, 14 beds; open June to end Sept (Tel 01 65 84
49 59; info@chaletvalferret.com; **www.chaletvalferret.
com**).

Take the path on the left-hand side of the building, and
climb above it to angle roughly southward across and up
the slope. The path forks and you continue on the upper
trail, now sweeping up the hillside in long loops to gain
another junction by an alp building. Turn right here along
what becomes an utterly delightful balcony path with
exquisite views to the Grandes Jorasses nearby, Aiguille
Noire de Peuterey and Mont Blanc de Courmayeur in
the middle distance, and Col de la Seigne far ahead.
It's a well-made, scenic route that crosses several minor
streams and is often flanked by alpenrose, bilberry or
larch.

After gaining a high point on a corner, the path
descends a little to another junction a few paces short
of the group of derelict alp buildings of Gioé (2007m).
Keep ahead and pass between the buildings to a view of
Rifugio Bonatti across a scoop of rough pasture. The trail
curves left, negotiates three streams, the second of which
comes crashing over a series of cascades (there's a good
footbridge), then approaches the simple alp buildings of
Malatra which stand on the slope just above

RIFUGIO BONATTI (15) (2025m, 5½–6hrs)
accommodation, refreshments; 85 dortoir places;
manned from March to April, and June to end of Sept;
(Tel 01 65 18 55 523; rifugiobonatti@gmail.com; **www.
rifugiobonatti.it**).

Opened in 1998 and named in honour of the great
Italian mountaineer Walter Bonatti, this is one of the
nicest and best-kept huts on the TMB, and with first-rate
facilities. The dining room looks downvalley to Mont
Blanc, while the Grandes Jorasses dominate the north
side of the valley directly opposite.

STAGE 3
Rifugio Bonatti – Courmayeur

Start point	Rifugio Bonatti (2025m)
Distance	12km (16km or 14km via Val Sapin *variantes 1 and 2*)
Height gain	120m (698m or 550m by the *variantes*)
Height loss	860m (1597m or 1449m)
Time	4hrs (4½–5hrs or 4–4½hrs via Val Sapin)
High point	Tête de la Tronche (2584m) (Mont de la Saxe option)
Accommodation	Le Pré (2½hrs) – privately-owned refuge (Rifugio Bertone)
Alternative routes	Col Sapin – Val Sapin – Villair
	Mont de la Saxe (see box on page 165)

Three ways are described to progress the route to Courmayeur; the newly rerouted TMB which cuts along the north flank of Mont de la Saxe, the former 'official' route along the crest of the Mont de la Saxe, and a *variante* descent from Col Sapin to Courmayeur. The first two are wonderful scenic routes, while the third is a bad-weather escape route. Given good, settled conditions, the new TMB and the former high trail vie with one another for superiority.

Main TMB Route

From the terrace beside Rifugio Bonatti descend on a signed path for a short distance to a junction, then turn left. The path cuts across the hillside and brings you to the buildings of Alp Sécheron. Pass immediately above these and continue across the hillside, passing through a belt of larches and rising to reach a signed junction in the tributary valley of Armina. Here you descend towards the ruins of Alp Arminaz (2033m), then swing left to a sturdy footbridge spanning the Torrent d'Armina.

Over the bridge the path now climbs out of Vallon d'Armina, and turning the spur soon enjoys ever-expanding views across and along the Val Ferret whose north wall is graced with a whole series of buttressed rock peaks, glaciers and domes of snow. As the walk progresses, the Brenva face of Mont Blanc, and the extraordinary spear-like Aiguille Noire come to dominate the unfolding scene.

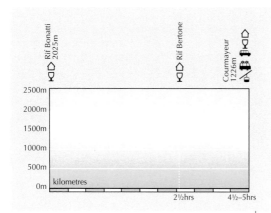

Twisting downhill, come to the long cattle byre of **ALP LÈCHE** (1929m) and then cut across pastures fluffed in places with cotton grass, to reach another path junction just above the ruins of Alp Leuchey. Ignoring these keep ahead on what is arguably the finest stretch of the day, for the path crosses a glorious open meadow and continues among light larchwoods that add to, rather than detract from the views. An undulating path, it climbs a little, loses height and rises again – always with tremendous panoramic views that threaten to delay all progress.

At the end of this stretch, the way rises again and is a little exposed – you can now see the Italian entrance to the Mont Blanc tunnel below – and then comes to yet another signed junction at about 2030m, where the Mont de la Saxe crest path option joins ours. Descend in a few minutes to the stone buildings of Le Pré and

RIFUGIO GIORGIO BERTONE (1989m, 2½hrs) accommodation, refreshments; 55 dortoir places, 14 beds; open mid-June to end Sept (Tel 01 65 84 46 12; info@rifugiobertone.it; **www.rifugiobertone.it**).

The path descends directly below the refuge, and from a bend shortly after there's another great view of Mont Blanc.

Most of the descent from here is through forest, some sections being fairly steep, and about 40mins from Rifugio Bertone you come onto a jeep track/dirt road at 1520m. This is the track taken by the alternative route from Col Sapin.

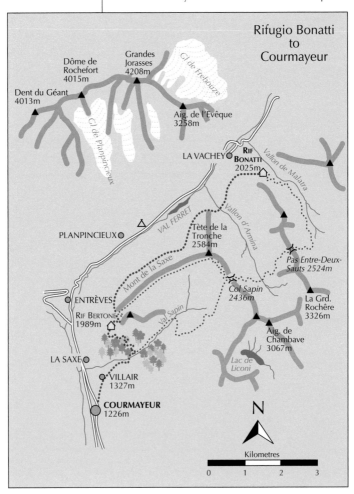

Rifugio Bonatti
to
Courmayeur

Dent du Géant
4013m

Dôme de
Rochefort
4015m

Grandes
Jorasses
4208m

Gl de Frebouze

Aig. de l'Evêque
3258m

Gl de Planpincieux

LA VACHEY

RIF
BONATTI
2025m

Vallon de Malatra

VAL FERRET

PLANPINCIEUX

Tête de la
Tronche
2584m

Vallon d'Armina

Pas Entre-Deux-
Sauts 2524m

Mont de la Saxe

Col Sapin
2436m

La Grd.
Rochère
3326m

ENTRÈVES

RIF BERTONE
1989m

Val Sapin

Aig. de
Chambave
3067m

LA SAXE

VILLAIR
1327m

Lac de
Liconi

COURMAYEUR
1226m

N

Kilometres

0   1   2   3

MONT DE LA SAXE OPTION

The long green crest of Mont de la Saxe

Ascend directly above the hut terrace to the Malatra alp buildings, where a sign at the right-hand end points you further up the hillside on a path with yellow waymarks. About 22mins from the rifugio come to Alpe supérieur de Malatra (2213m). A few paces before the first of the buildings the path forks. Take the right branch, which shortly brings you to a level pasture with streams meandering through, and the Grande Rochêre to the south.

Coming to another junction of paths, go ahead through the Vallon de Malatra; an easy walk with alpine flowers in the pastures or clustered among wayside rocks. Towards the head of the valley the path curves to the right, rising across grass slopes to gain the **Pas Entre-Deux-Sauts** (2524m, 1¼hrs). From this broad saddle Mont Blanc appears to the west, while across the head of the Vallon d'Armina the path to Col Sapin shows as a clearly defined scar across the hillside.

The way down to the head of Vallon d'Armina is undemanding, and on grass slopes virtually all the way. In the valley head several streams are crossed, with stepping stones across the most boisterous – caution is needed when the water level is high. The lowest point between Pas Entre-Deux-Sauts and Col Sapin is reached where another path descends to the right (2285m). Looking down through the valley once again the Grandes Jorasses dominate.

The ascent to Col Sapin takes a little under 25mins from the Vallon d'Armina path junction. **Col Sapin** (2436m, 2hrs) is a neat dip in a ridge spur connecting Tête de la Tronche and Tête du Curru; there's a signpost and a junction of paths on the col. The Mont de la Saxe route climbs steeply to the right, but the easier alternative (see box opposite) which should be used in poor visibility or bad weather descends through Val Sapin.

Turn right and climb a short but very steep slope up the flank of Tête de la Tronche, soon gaining a view left through Val Sapin to the toy-like buildings of Courmayeur. The grass crown of the Tête at 2684m is gained in about 15–20mins, and the panorama is impressive. This is a classic viewpoint, and it's worth spending a few minutes here to absorb it all.

The continuing route runs along the crest of Mont de la Saxe with those views to absorb all the way. It comes as no surprise to find that Edward Whymper and his guides chose to visit this crest in June 1865 in order to study the Grandes Jorasses prior to making its ascent. From here the mountain can be scrutinised in all its fine detail. First sloping down to a little saddle below the Tête Bernarda (views onto La Vachey and up to the Grand Col Ferret), the path then goes along the crest where a number of little pools act as mirrors to reflect the mountains. When the path unravels into several strands, it's best to remain on the ridge top, which provides easy walking. Soon after passing avalanche fences the path cuts through a narrow grassy 'gully' and then begins the descent to Rifugio Bertone and Courmayeur. At first gentle, the slope suddenly steepens dramatically until you're looking directly onto the rooftops of Le Pré.

At the foot of this steep slope come to a junction of paths; the right-hand option being the main TMB from Rifugio Bonatti, but the TMB veers left and an easy 5mins later comes to the chalets of Le Pré and **Rifugio Giorgio Bertone** (1970m, 3½hrs – see page 163 for details).

Turn right, and about 50m later take an unmarked path on the left, descending among trees to shortcut a long loop in the track. Rejoining the track, turn left and wander down to **Villair** (1327m, 3½hrs), an attractive village of neat stone houses. Walk through the village, and at a T-junction veer slightly left ahead and arrive 5mins later by the church in

COURMAYEUR (1226m) hotels, pensions, restaurants, banks, ATM, shops, PTT. Tourist information: AIAT Monte Bianco, Piazzale Monte Bianco 13, Courmayeur (Tel 01 65 84 20 60; courmayer@turismo.vda.it; **www.lovevda.it**) Lower-priced accommodation: Pensione Venezia (Tel 01 65 84 24 61); Hotel Select

TMB VARIANTE: VAL SAPIN – VILLAIR

From Val Sapin take the signed path ahead, which descends a little west of south in zigzags to a stream crossing under the Tête du Curru. Over this the way goes to the alp buildings of **Curru** (1964m), then to another stream where the path forks. Take the right branch (the left-hand alternative climbs to Col de Liconi) and keep right again at the next fork, where an optional route to Courmayeur goes via La Suche, while the TMB preferred path descends to the valley bed near Chapy on the right bank of the Sapin stream. Keeping on the right bank wander downvalley to **La Trappe** (1505m), a huddle of buildings on a jeep track which is joined soon after by the main TMB path descending from the right. About 50m beyond this take an unmarked path on the left, which drops among trees and shortcuts a loop in the road, which it rejoins lower down. Turn left and follow the road down to **Villair** (2hrs from Col Sapin).

(Tel 01 65 84 66 61; select@courmayeurhotel.com; **www.courmayeurhotel.com**); Hotel Edelweiss (Tel 01 65 84 15 90; info@albergoedelweiss.it); Hotel Svizzero (Tel 01 65 84 81 70; info@hotelsvizzero.com; **www.hotelsvizzero.com**); Hotel Crampon (Tel 01 65 84 23 85 info@crampon.it; **www.crampon.it**).

The town has a bright and welcoming face, and the traffic-free streets leading from the square in front of the church have plenty of restaurants and shops in which to spend your money. The tourist office is located further down the slope in a large building overlooking the large Piazzale Monte Bianco – to find it please see directions for the start of Stage 4. From practically every street the big mountains are on display to the north.

If you plan to have a day off in Courmayeur, the weather is clear and you have sufficient funds, consider riding the Funivie Monte Bianco (cablecar) from La Palud to Pointe Hellbronner at 3462m for tremendous high mountain views. It's then possible to continue by gondola across 5km of the glaciated Vallée Blanche to the Aiguille du Midi (above Chamonix) and back again; a truly memorable experience.

Note Should you need to cut short your circuit, buses run daily through the Mont Blanc Tunnel to Chamonix.

STAGE 4
Courmayeur – Rifugio Elisabetta

Start point	Courmayeur (1226m)
Distance	18km
Height gain	1560m
Height loss	460m
Time	4½–5hrs
High point	Mont Favre spur (2430m)
Transport options	Cablecar (Courmayeur – Plan Chécrouit)
	Bus (Courmayeur – La Visaille)
Accommodation	Dolonne (10 mins) – hotels
	Col Chécrouit (2hrs) – gîte-refuge
	Lac Combal (3½–4hrs) – gîte-refuge
	Rifugio Elisabetta
Alternative route	By way of Val Veni all the way to Rifugio Elisabetta – a bad-weather 'escape' route.

Heading southwest away from Courmayeur the TMB takes a high route above the Val Veni, where, from Col Chécrouit almost as far as Lac Combal, a tremendous balcony path reveals the spectacularly disordered south side of the Mont Blanc range to match the panorama gained on Stage 3 along the flank (or crest) of Mont de la Saxe. The two stages complement one another with similarities, yet each is unique in its own way.

Since a good part of this route is over high, open country without shelter, it should be avoided in the likelihood of storms. In the case of bad weather, perhaps the best option is to take the bus (from the square in front of Courmayeur tourist office) to La Visaille in Val Veni, walk up the continuing road to Lac Combal, then follow directions to Rifugio Elisabetta given in the final paragraph of the route description.

Standing in the square overlooking the valley with your back to the church, turn left and immediately across the square descend a flight of steps on the right until you reach a crossing road opposite the Biverbanca. Cross straight ahead and walk down to a roundabout on the edge of the Piazzale Monte Bianco. (To the right you'll

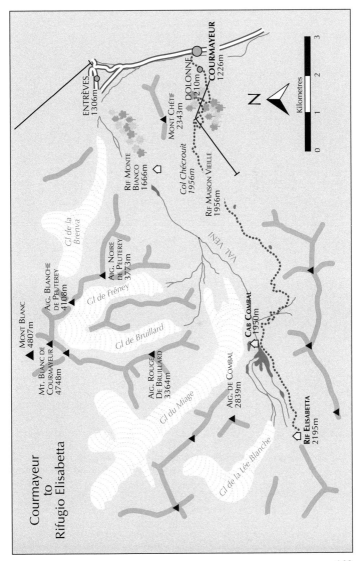

Courmayeur
to
Rifugio Elisabetta

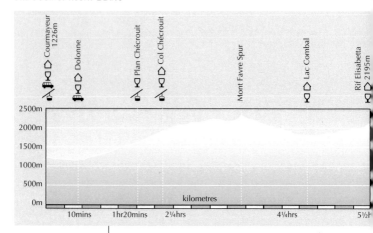

find a drinking water supply, public telephones, toilets, tourist office, PTT and bus station.) Go ahead, then half-right (sign to Dolonne) and walk beneath a road bridge. Beyond the bridge cross the Doire Baltéa river, noting the splendid view to the right where the Aiguille (or Dent) du Géant raises a rocky finger above a glacial cirque. The way now curves left, rising towards

DOLONNE (1210m, 10mins, accommodation, refreshments)

Turn right on a minor road leading to Hotel Ottoz and go between buildings to the main street, Via della Vittoria, where you turn left. Here, at the heart of Dolonne, the village is seen to be crowded with attractive stone houses displaying flowers at their windows and balconies, the old buildings that squeeze alleyways and narrow streets having been renovated and prettified. Despite 'gentrification' the village remains utterly charming.

When the main street forks take the right branch, Via Mont Chétif, which becomes Strada Chécrouit near the village washplace. Out of Dolonne keep ahead along the narrow road rising between meadows towards a small valley. At the top of the first meadow turn right onto the Sentiero Olivier Ottoz, a narrow path signed to Plan Chécrouit. After a brief contour, the path twists up the steep wooded slope, and onto a dirt road where you turn right. The continuing path maintains its steep course among trees, and eventually climbs some steps to reach a junction of paths. Turn left along a narrow section leading to the Funivia Courmayeur (cablecar station). Walk ahead on a dirt road, then cut right onto another track/dirt road winding uphill. Keep alert for a TMB sign which directs you onto a path climbing grass slopes on the right. Reaching ski tows and buildings bear left along another dirt road, shortly after which you come to the

RIFUGIO LE RANDONNEUR (1890m) 25 dortoir places and beds; open from mid-June to end of Sept (Tel 349 53 68 898; info@randonneurmb.com; **www.**randonneurmb.com).

A short distance beyond the gîte take a piste on the right which rises up a grass slope. Near the head of the slope pass along the right-hand side of a ski tow and come to a junction of tracks. Walk ahead to **Col Chécrouit** and the privately-owned

RIFUGIO MAISON VIEILLE (1956m, 1hr 50mins) 50 dortoir places; open from mid-June to end Sept (Tel 337 23 09 79; info@maisonvieille.com; **www.**maisonvieille.com).

The Maison Vieille enjoys a privileged position with a direct view across the valley to the armchair-like hollow known as the Fauteuil des Allemands (the 'German armchair') on the face of the Aiguille Noire de Peuterey, while to the south distant outliers of the Gran Paradiso range can be seen through the narrows of Val d'Aosta.

Turn left alongside the restaurant on a rising path towards trees. This is the start of the balcony walk, where the TMB makes its way along the hillside with a magical panorama unfolding with each step. Sometimes among

The high path above Val Veni provides stunning views throughout

trees, but more often across open slopes, the path climbs, eases, then rises again, and as you make progress so the trail passes a few small pools that add a sparkle to the landscape.

About 1¼hrs beyond Col Chécrouit cross a grassy bluff, then descend a little into a combe where a stream has cut a groove in the lip of hillside, forcing the way onto a few stepping stones. After this the path rises again, and with a few zigzags tops the highest part of the walk (2430m) on a spur pushing northward from Mont Favre. From this high point the full length of both Val Veni **(12)** below and Val Ferret to the northeast can be seen, as can Rifugio Elisabetta nestling below the Aiguille des Glaciers to the west. Mont Blanc is directly across the valley, guarded by abrupt rock walls and drained by the Miage and Brenva glaciers.

Descend easily on the west side of the spur, and about 12mins below the high point note another little pool in a grassy hollow below the path on the left. In the early summer this nestles among a riot of alpine flowers. Continuing down, pass the abandoned stone hutment of Alpe supérieure de l'Arp Vieille (2303m) and go down the right-hand side of a cascading stream. Stepping stones eventually carry the path across to the left, then down to more ruins, the former Alpe inférieur de l'Arp Vieille, and 7mins later you'll come onto a stony track in the bed of the Val Veni by the huge wall of lateral moraine deposited by the Miage glacier (1950m, 3½–4hrs). Nearby lie the milky blue waters of Lac Combal.

Nearby stands the **Cabane du Combal** (1950m 3½–4hrs) 23 dorm places, open June to September (Tel 01 65 17 56 421; cabaneducombal@gmail.com).

Turn left along the track and follow it almost all the way to the refuge, which is reached in about 1hr from here. It's a pleasant walk through the near-level Vallon de la Lée Blanche (the upper reaches of Val Veni), the bed of a large glacial lake at the time of de Saussure's visit, whose sole remnant today is the complex of streams and marshes of Lac Combal. Ahead can be seen the sharply tilted Pyramides Calcaires, a limestone anomaly on the edge of a granite massif, with the much higher Aiguille des Glaciers above and to the right of these, whose glaciers tumble down towards Rifugio Elisabetta. When the track rises in long loops you'll notice footpath shortcuts which lead eventually to the buildings of Alpe infériure de la Lée Blanche, once a military barracks. A final path cuts uphill from here to the

RIFUGIO ELISABETTA (2195m, 4½–5hrs) accommodation, refreshments; 53 dortoir places, 20 beds; manned mid-June to mid-Sept (Tel 01 65 84 40 80; info@rifugioelisabetta.com). Owned and staffed by the Milan section of the CAI the rifugio, officially named Elisabetta Soldini, overlooks the lower Vallon de la Lée Blanche from a spur extending from one of the Pyramides Calcaires, and is backed by the Glaciers d'Estellette and de la Lée Blanche. Sunset views can be magical.

STAGE 5
Rifugio Elisabetta – Refuge de la Croix du Bonhomme

Start point	Rifugio Elisabetta (2195m)
Distance	20km (or 16km via Col des Fours *variante*)
Height gain	1147m (or 1134m)
Height loss	1004m (or 949m)
Time	5½–6hrs
High point	Col de la Seigne 2516m (or Col des Fours (2665m))
Accommodation	Les Mottets (2¼hrs) – privately-owned refuge
	Les Chapieux (3½hrs) – auberge/refuge, camping
	Col de la Croix – CAF refuge
Alternative route	Ville des Glaciers – Col des Fours – Refuge de la Croix (see below)

An undemanding climb to Col de la Seigne starts the day well, and if the weather is kind and you don't delay departure from the hut, you should be on the Franco-Italian border early enough to catch the crisp morning views that are so splendid from this high point. Col de la Seigne is the counterbalance to the Grand Col Ferret crossed three days ago, but, if anything, the panorama gained from it is even better than that from the earlier pass. On the French side of the col the TMB descends into the little Vallée des Glaciers, where the dairy-farm-turned-refuge of Les Mottets lies at the foot of the slope. Shortly after this, at the Ville des Glaciers, the way forks. One route climbs to Col des Fours (see box below) which, along with the Fenêtre d'Arpette (crossed on Alternative Stage 10), is the highest point reached on the TMB. The other continues down through the valley to Les Chapieux, a small hamlet at the southernmost limit of the circuit. From there a path climbs steadily to the large Refuge de la Croix du Bonhomme, built just below the col after which it is named.

Descend a little from Rifugio Elisabetta on a narrow path that cuts rounds to the right then slopes down to join a broader path leading through the pastures of the Vallon de la Lée Blanche. Along here it's worth pausing to enjoy a backward view to the spear-like Aiguille Noire

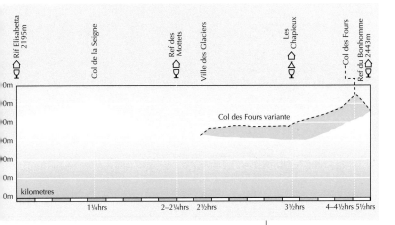

At top of profile, left to right:
Rif Elisabetta 2195m · Col de la Seigne · Ref des Mottets · Ville des Glaciers · Les Chapieux · Col des Fours · Ref du Bonhomme 2443m

Col des Fours variante

kilometres

1¼hrs · 2–2¼hrs · 2½hrs · 3½hrs · 4–4½hrs · 5½hrs

de Peuterey, a truly dramatic gesticulating rock spire. For
the first 15mins the way through the pastures is level, but
then you begin to rise towards the col, passing the solitary building of La Casermetta (2365m) that once served
as the Italian customs house, and has now been refurbished and made into a museum and mountain information centre (45–50mins). The way continues to climb
without too much effort, although the final slopes may
well be covered with late-lying snow or even patches
of ice, in which case caution is advised. About 20mins
beyond the customs house you arrive at the broad **Col de
la Seigne (11)** (2516m, 1¼hrs), marked by a large cairn
and an orientation table in place of the simple shelter and
a cross that used to stand here.

At first the view ahead into France is limited, but the
Italian side of Mont Blanc is so magnificent that it's worth
spending time here to savour it. Unless your intention is
to take the Col des Fours *variante*, this will be your last
opportunity to study the mountain for another two days.
And then it will look somewhat different. But Mont Blanc
is only part of a truly splendid panorama which includes
much of the route you've been following for the past two
or three days, and it will be entertaining trying to identify

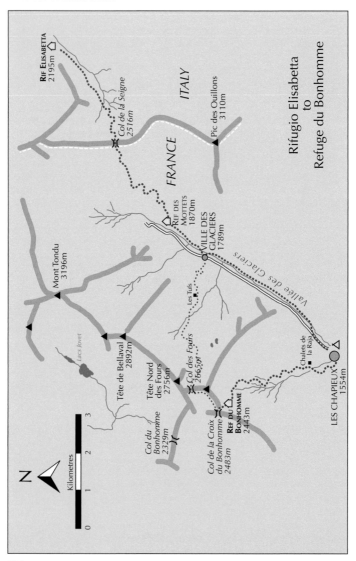

RIF ELISABETTA
2195m

ITALY

Col de la Seigne
2516m

Pic des Ouillons
3110m

FRANCE

REF DES MOTTETS
1870m

Mont Tondu
3196m

VILLE DES GLACIERS
1789m

Vallée des Glaciers

Les Tufs

Lacs Jovet

Tête de Bellaval
2892m

Tête Nord des Fours
2756m

Col des Fours
2665m

Chalets de la Raja

LES CHAPIEUX
1554m

Col du Bonhomme
2329m

Col de la Croix du Bonhomme
2483m

REF DU BONHOMME
2443m

Rifugio Elisabetta
to
Refuge du Bonhomme

N
Kilometres
0   1   2   3

176

individual sections of the TMB, as well as putting names to peaks that have become familiar from different angles.

On the descent into France the convex slope of the col delays full observation of the Vallée des Glaciers **(10)** for several minutes, but when the path curves left an unobstructed view shows the way down to Les Chapieux, where the valley then curves sharply to the south and disappears. The huddled buildings of the Ville des Glaciers are a good focal point. It is there that the way divides, and in good visibility the twisting path of the Col des Fours route can be seen climbing the steep hillside above that hamlet.

Descent to Refuge des Mottets is pleasant – on a mostly good path angling across steep grass slopes with a couple of minor streams to negotiate on the way to it.

The Vallée des Glaciers spreads in a hint of shadow below Col de la Seigne

REFUGE DES MOTTETS (1870m, 2–2¼hrs) accommodation, refreshments; 90 dortoir places; open mid-June to mid-Sept (Tel 04 79 07 01 70; www.lesmottets.com).

This former dairy farm has been adapted for overnight accommodation, using the cowsheds for

Once a dairy farm, Refuge des Mottets now provides accommodation for TMB walkers below Col de la Seigne

dormitories, and the dining room in the main building being decorated with an assortment of old cheese-making and farming implements. Some evenings the guardienne entertains with music on her accordion.

A short distance beyond the refuge cross a stream on a footbridge, and a few paces after this join a track. When it curves to cross a bridge below the farming hamlet of **La Ville des Glaciers** (1789m; water supply and toilet block), take a footpath heading downvalley, still on the left bank of the Torrent des Glaciers. However, should it be your plan to take the Col des Fours *variante*, cross the bridge, go up the slope to the buildings and follow directions as below.

Main Route via Les Chapieux
Follow the left bank footpath heading downstream. Shortly before reaching Les Chapieux, it crosses the river then climbs above the road for a while before sloping down onto the road leading into the hamlet of

LES CHAPIEUX (1554, 3½hrs) accommodation, refreshments in Auberge de la Nova (35 dortoir places, 35 beds; open May to end Oct (Tel 04 79 89 07 15; info@refugelanova.com); Chambres du Soleil, 14 beds (Tel 04 79 31 22; lesoleildeschapieux@gmail.com; camping permitted in meadows below the hamlet – public toilet block next to seasonal tourist office; small grocery.

TMB VARIANTE:
COL DES FOURS – REFUGE DE LA CROIX DU BONHOMME

This route should only be attempted if the weather is settled, visibility is good and conditions are favourable on the ground. Col des Fours is high and relatively remote, and often snowbound into mid-summer. It is, however, more direct than the standard Les Chapieux route, and will appeal to experienced mountain walkers. Before leaving Ville des Glaciers, do not neglect to top up your water bottle from the standpipe.

The way begins by following the track/dirt road which rises up the hillside above La Ville des Glaciers to the alp of Les Tufs (1993m) in about 30mins. Leave the track on a path which cuts off by some cowsheds, contouring left to a stream. Across this the way then climbs along its left-hand side to gain a bluff, continues towards a cascade and climbs steeply again to a level area at the foot of a slope of shale and, possibly, snow patches. The final ascent to Col des Fours tackles this shale slope, which seems unremittingly steep, and about 1¾–2hrs after leaving La Ville des Glaciers you emerge onto the barren saddle of **Col des Fours** (2665m, 4–4½hrs).

The classic viewpoint of the 2756m Tête Nord des Fours (8) is easily accessible from here in a 40min round-trip. Bear half-right (northwest) at the col and follow a line of cairns up the ridge for 20–25mins to reach an orientation table on the modest summit. The 360° panoramic view definitely makes this diversion worthwhile.

For Col de la Croix du Bonhomme and the refuge, turn left (SSW) at Col des Fours to cross the west flank of Tête Sud des Fours, then slope down to an electricity pylon. Continue ahead, now along the ridge crest as far as a large cairn on the 2483m **Col de la Croix du Bonhomme**. Turn left and follow the path down a short distance to the **Refuge de la Croix du Bonhomme** (9) (2443m, 4½–5hrs). See refuge details in the main text for this stage.

The path to the Bonhomme refuge leaves Les Chapieux directly opposite Auberge de la Nova, where a sign suggests it will take 2hrs for the ascent. Climbing to a grass track the way swings up the hillside with footpath shortcuts, and after a few bends the track forks. Take the right branch, crossing a stream and looping up to a stony crossing track. Turn right and walk along this for 6mins, then break off to the right over a bridge towards the **Chalets de la Raja** (1789m).

Immediately take a path on the left to climb straight up the grass slope for another 30mins or so before drawing level with more alp buildings, the **Chalets de Plan Varraro** (2006m, 4½hrs), from which the refuge can be seen on what appears to be a broad saddle at the head of the valley. Although it does not appear to be an hour's walk away – it is. As you continue, so the refuge dips out of sight, and the path twists up a steepening slope, crosses a number of streams, then veers left across rolling grassy bluffs to suddenly find

REFUGE DE LA CROIX DU BONHOMME (9)

(2443m, 5½hrs) accommodation, refreshments; 113 dortoir places; manned mid-June to mid-Sept (Tel 04 79 07 05 28; refuge-bonhomme@free.fr).

An unusual-looking building, the original stone structure was given timber additions when the CAF took it over in the 1990s. Solar panels power the hot-water system, so if you arrive on a dull day, don't expect to enjoy 10 minutes under a steaming shower! The refuge faces south and commands a big panorama. The eye-catching peak seen in the distance is Mont Pourri.

STAGE 6
Refuge de la Croix du Bonhomme – Les Contamines

Start point	Refuge de la Croix du Bonhomme (2443m)
Distance	13km
Height gain	40m
Height loss	1316m
Time	3–3½hrs
High point	Col de la Croix du Bonhomme (2483m)
Transport option	Bus (Notre-Dame de la Gorge – Les Contamines)
Accommodation	La Balme (1½hrs) – chalet/gîte
	Nant-Borrant (2–2¼hrs) – refuge
	Pontet (2½–3hrs) – gîte, camping
	Les Contamines – hotels, dortoirs, gîte
Route options	Detours to Tête Nord des Fours and Lacs Jovet

This is a short and easy walk, downhill nearly all the way, and it would be possible to take a bite out of tomorrow's route by going beyond Les Contamines as far as the Gîte du Champel or Auberge du Truc, perhaps, but it would be a shame to do so. On its own this walk has plenty to enjoy, but there are temptations to stray away from the route too, to visit the classic viewpoint of Tête Nord des Fours (for those who came via Les Chapieux yesterday) and (from the Plan Jovet above La Balme) to make a detour as far as the idyllic Lacs Jovet. Either or both these options will add something special to the TMB experience.

At the end of the day Les Contamines-Montjoie is a cheerful little resort with lots of accommodation, a few restaurants, supermarkets and a bank, and it makes a pleasant overnight stay.

Behind the refuge the path to **Col de la Croix du Bonhomme** (2483m) is clearly defined, and it takes little more than 5mins to reach the saddle with its junction of paths. The route of the TMB crosses over and descends northward, but the right-hand path suggests a diversion to the Tête Nord des Fours **(8)** viewpoint – a round-trip of 1½–2hrs (see box below).

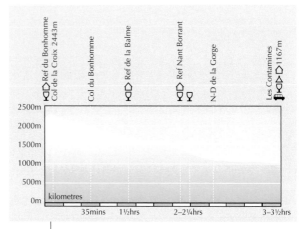

Descend to a stream below the north side of Col de la Croix du Bonhomme, crossing as you do the boundary of the Réserve Naturelle des Contamines-Montjoie (7). Over the stream the TMB path veers west and northwest over rocky terrain for a while, then down to the **Col du Bonhomme** (2329m, 35mins) on which there's a small timber-built emergency shelter and, in good conditions, long views through the Val Montjoie to the north, with the Vallon de la Gittaz in the south.

OPTIONAL DETOUR TO TÊTE NORD DES FOURS

Turn right (northeast) at the Col de la Croix du Bonhomme and follow the path which rises along an easy crest as far as an electricity pylon. After this the way cuts along the left flank of Tête Sud des Fours, on the far side of which lies the bare saddle of Col des Fours – the TMB *variante* link with La Ville des Glaciers (see Stage 5). This is reached in about 30mins from Col de la Croix. A line of cairns now directs the route along the left side of the ridge working northwest, then northeast along the crest itself – there's a great view into the upper Val Montjoie and onto the Lacs Jovet below to the left, while Mont Blanc appears directly ahead above and behind the Aiguilles des Glaciers and Tré la Tête. Gained in about 15–20mins from Col

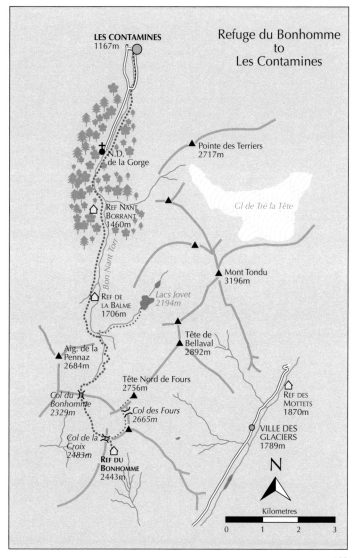

LES CONTAMINES
1167m

Refuge du Bonhomme
to
Les Contamines

N.D.
de la Gorge

Pointe des Terriers
2717m

Gl de Tré la Tête

REF NANT
BORRANT
1460m

Mont Tondu
3196m

Bon Nant Torr

REF DE
LA BALME
1706m

Lacs Jovet
2194m

Aig. de la
Pennaz
2684m

Tête de
Bellaval
2892m

Tête Nord de Fours
2756m

REF DES
MOTTETS
1870m

Col du
Bonhomme
2329m

Col des Fours
2665m

VILLE DES
GLACIERS
1789m

Col de la
Croix
2483m

REF DU
BONHOMME
2443m

N

Kilometres

0   1   2   3

183

des Fours, the **Tête Nord des Fours** (2756m) is hardly a summit, more a high point on the ridge topped by an orientation table. However, the vast 360° panoramic view is tremendous, and is recognised as being one of the finest accessible to walkers on this side of the massif. Return to Col de la Croix du Bonhomme by the same route.

Bear right and descend steeply into the head of the Bon Nant glen (the upper reaches of Val Montjoie) – the path consists of many strands, all leading down to the Plan des Dames, where you come to a large conical pile of stones said to mark the spot where an English woman perished in a storm. Just beyond this the way is squeezed between rocks before descending to the next valley level, the Plan Jovet. The path divides here, but re-forms a little later. Streams meander through flowery meadows, and there are a few marshy areas. On coming to a track/dirt road another path breaks to the right, signed to the Lacs Jovet in 45mins.

Given sufficient time and energy – and decent weather – it would be worth straying up to the lakes, maybe for a picnic (see box below).

OPTIONAL DETOUR TO THE LACS JOVET

Take the signed path heading off to the right, which soon forks. Take the right branch to cross a stream coming from a waterfall that cascades down from the hanging valley where the Lacs Jovet are found. The path rises towards the waterfall among alpenrose, juniper and bilberry shrubs, curves away from it, then angles up to a lip of hillside over which you enter an upper basin of meadows. A short distance further along the path and you reach the first and larger of the **Lacs Jovet** at 2174m (45mins). Rising behind the lake is Mont Tondu, but the best views are to be gained from the north shore looking back. Paths edge both east and west shorelines, and a circuit of the lake will take about 20–25mins. The second lake lies in a hollow at the far end of the first and about 20m higher. There are also a couple of small pools lodged on the east side of the main lake. Return by the same path to the track in the Plan Jovet to rejoin the TMB.

One of the Lacs Jovet reached by recommended diversion above Refuge de la Balme

The height gain is about 250m, and you should allow at least 2hrs for this detour in order to make a circuit of the larger of the two lakes and return to the TMB path.

Follow the track on the left-hand side of the Bon Nant stream for about 2mins, then break away on a signed stony path on the right which descends steeply down a rough hillside before rejoining the track just above the

REFUGE DE LA BALME (1706m, 1½hrs) accommodation, refreshments; 36 dortoir places, 14 beds; open mid-June to mid-Sept (Tel 04 50 47 03 54).

About 1min below this, note the public toilet block and a water supply on the right. About 100m to the left there's a small site (*emplacement de bivouac*) where overnight camping is permitted. Keep to the track all the way down through the valley which from Col du Bonhomme descends in a series of natural steps. Below the refuge you wander between pastures and patches of woodland, and 30mins from La Balme a second track breaks to the right, leading in 100m to another emplacement de

The tranquil reaches of Val Montjoie spread away from Refuge de la Balme

bivouac. Keeping to the main valley track, in a little over 5mins you come to the attractive

REFUGE NANT BORRANT (1460m, 2–2¼hrs) accommodation, refreshments; 35 dortoir places; open early June to late Sept (Tel 04 50 47 03 57 refugenantborrant@free.fr).

Just 2mins beyond the refuge pass the **Alpinus Lodge** (*refreshments*) and descend into forest. The way takes you over a fine old arched bridge, then steepens on the final drop to the valley floor, which is gained just to the right of the impressive pilgrimage chapel of **Notre-Dame de la Gorge (6)** (1210m). A path cuts off to visit the chapel, which has a café-restaurant next door.

The TMB approach to Les Contamines remains on the right bank of the stream. When the way forks take the broad path on the right. Along this stretch which leads to the main road, note a small lake on the left, and signs to the campsite (Camping Le Pontet). This also has a gîte – see details under Les Contamines at the end of this stage.

On reaching the main road where it makes a sharp bend to cross the Bon Nant, keep ahead for a short distance until a sign directs you onto a path slanting left into trees, signed to Les Contamines Centre. At first on the right bank, it soon crosses to the stream's left bank. For accommodation at the comfortable **Chalet-Hotel La Chemenaz** (Tel 04 50 47 02 44) walk up the road for about 2mins, otherwise continue on the river's left bank path, which 10mins later brings you over a footbridge and up a slope to the main road at the southern end of **Les Contamines-Montjoie (5)**. Continue ahead to find the tourist office, shops and so on in the heart of the village.

LES CONTAMINES-MONTJOIE (1167m, 3–3½hrs) Office de tourisme (Tel 04 50 47 01 58; info@lescontamines.com); hotels, pensions, dortoirs, gîte, CAF refuge, camping; restaurants, shops, bank, ATM, PTT, bus link with St-Gervais-les-Bains. Lower-priced accommodation: Refuge du CAF, 28 dortoir places, open mid-June to mid-Sept (Tel 04 50 47 00 88); Chalet Bonaventure, 8 dortoir places, open mid-June to mid-Sept (Tel 04 50 47 23 53; camille.bonaventure@wanadoo.fr); Hotel Christiania, beds (Tel 04 50 47 02 72 hotel-christiania@wanadoo.fr; **www.lescontamines.com/hotel-lechristiania**). The Gîte Le Pontet is located at Camping Le Pontet (Tel 04 50 47 04 04; campingdupontet@wanadoo.fr), 2km south of the village near N.D. de la Gorge; 32 dortoir places, open June to late Sept. For complete hotel details contact the tourist office

STAGE 7
Les Contamines – Bionnassay – Les Houches

Start point	Les Contamines (1167m)
Distance	16km
Height gain	633m
Height loss	646m
Time	4½hrs
High point	Col de Voza (1653m)
Transport options	Bus (Les Contamines – Tresse – St Gervais)
	Train (St Gervais – Col de Voza)
	Cableway (Bellevue – Les Houches)
Accommodation	Le Champel (1½hrs) – gîte
	Bionnassay (2¼hrs) – gîte
	Chalet-Refuge du Fioux (2¾hrs) – gîte
	Col de Voza (3hrs) –hotel
	Les Houches – hotels, dortoirs, gîte, camping
Alternative route	Les Contamines – Col de Voza via Refuge de Miage and Col de Tricot (see Alternative Stage 7)

The particular route via Bionnassay described here may not have the big mountain grandeur associated with its alternative, but it is a very pleasant stage all the same. On this walk habitation is as important as a backdrop of glaciers and rock walls, and, by contrast with the previous four stages, there are rather fewer footpaths than tracks or minor service roads. The two routes come together on Col de Voza for a united descent into Les Houches in the Vallée de l'Arve.

From the car park below the tourist office in the centre of Les Contamines, take the footpath which slants downhill among trees and brings you to a riverside path where you bear right. Keeping the river on your left follow this footpath all the way to a road bridge, Pont de Moulin, which is reached after about 18mins. Cross the bridge and fork right by a timber yard on a lane signed to Les Hoches. About 50m later take a turning on the right, a narrow

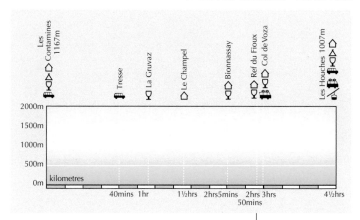

road cutting between meadows to **Les Hoches** (25mins), a hamlet of chalets and farm buildings where the astronomer Alexis Bouvard was born in 1767. Rising between buildings the road forks. Take the right-hand option, which soon becomes a track leading through a strip of woodland. When it forks by a house take the lower path and very shortly arrive in **Le Quy**, about 9mins from Les Hoches. Coming to a narrow metalled road walk ahead and follow it downhill, over the river and up to the main D902 road at **Tresse** (1020m, 40mins).

Cross directly ahead and walk along the Chemin de Tresse, which takes you through the two-part village divided by meadows. On reaching the last house, about 7mins from the road, a path on the right climbs into forest and 9mins later emerges by the entrance to the Gorges de la Gruvaz. These gorges (entrance fee payable) have been cut by the Miage torrent, which carries the meltwater from glaciers suspended from the Dômes de Miage, seen to such good effect on the Alternative Stage.

Turn left here, cross to a car park and wander along the road into the village of **La Gruvaz** (1hr). Immediately after passing a water trough, take a track descending on the right. Emerging at a minor crossroads below the village, turn right along the narrow Chemin de la Fontaine,

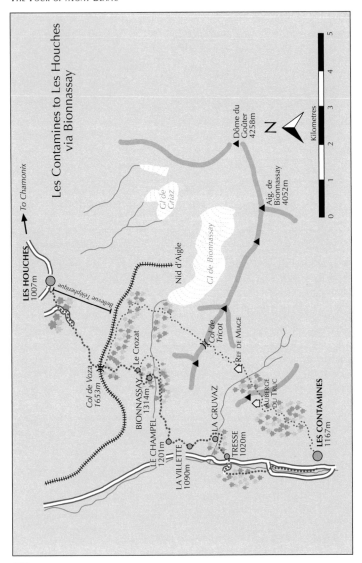

Les Contamines to Les Houches
via Bionnassay

To Chamonix

Dôme du Goûter
4258m

Gl de Griaz

Aig. de
Bionnassay
4052m

Nid d'Aigle

Gl de Bionnassay

LES HOUCHES
1007m

Bellevue Téléphérique

Col de
Tricot

REF DE MIAGE

Col de Voza
1653m

Le Crozat

BIONNASSAY
1314m

AUBERGE
DU TRUC

LE CHAMPEL
1201m

LA GRUVAZ

TRESSE
1020m

LA VILLETTE
1090m

LES CONTAMINES
1167m

N

Kilometres

0 1 2 3 4 5

190

which leads between farmland dotted with attractive chalets and farms to a junction of lanes by a large water trough in **LA VILLETTE** (1090m).

Bear right, and in another 40m take a track on the right by a building (direction Le Champel and Col de Voza). This rises through more meadows and woodland, steeply at times, before joining another road at the entrance to **LE CHAMPEL** (1201, 1½hrs), a neat hamlet of old houses, with the

> **GÎTE DU CHAMPEL** 8 dortoir places, 34 beds; open June to mid-Sept (Tel 04 50 47 77 55; gîte@champel.fr). See also **LE PECLET**, another gîte with six places in two rooms; open June to end September (Tel 06 84 18 45 55; lepeclet@orange.fr).

Before walking up the road into the hamlet, pause to enjoy the fine view back through the Val Montjoie **(4)** to the distant Col du Bonhomme. Resuming the walk, note that when the road swings sharply to the right, the gîte is just off to the left. Soon after, pass a little chapel whose altar is made of logs, and just before leaving the hamlet there's an opportunity to top up water bottles at a spring-fed trough.

Out of Le Champel a track/dirt road makes a gently rising traverse of the steep and wooded south flank of the Bionnassay valley. Before entering woodland there's a view left to St Gervais-les-Bains. A little under 30mins along this track, come to a signed footpath junction and a choice of onward routes. The TMB takes the footpath option to Bionnassay, then goes up a road then track to Col de Voza. The alternative is to stay on the track which joins the main TMB near Le Crozat. Both options are described.

Main TMB Route via Bionnassay

Turn left on the footpath which descends steeply to cross a footbridge over a glacial torrent, then climbs through more woodland to a road at **Bionnassay** (1314m, 2hrs 5mins; *accommodation, refreshments*), a small hamlet nestling just above the narrows of the Bionnassay valley, with overnight accommodation at the

ROUTE OPTION VIA LE CROZAT

Remain on the track, which rises and crosses three forest clearings. At the end of the third clearing the track swings left, loses a little height to cross the Torrent de Bionnassay, then rises once more. Passing a solitary stone house continue a little further, then bear right at a junction by a wooden chalet, and shortly after you'll reach the collection of farm buildings of **Le Crozat** (2hrs 25mins); one of the farms has local goat cheese for sale. Here the track brings you onto the crossing road which links Bionnassay with Col de Voza, where you rejoin the TMB.

AUBERGE DE BIONNASSAY 27 dortoir places, 18 beds; open June to end Sept (Tel 04 50 93 45 23).

As you come into the hamlet at a hairpin bend the gîte is a few paces to the left. For the continuing route walk up the road and soon pass a café, then a *buvette* (La Barmette), both on the right, and several minutes later note the farming hamlet of Le Crozat, also on the right, with a brief view of the Aiguille de Bionnassay as a backdrop. The metalled road ends at a parking area, and a jeep track/dirt road continues into more open country to allow splendid views to be gained of the Aiguilles de Bionnassay and du Goûter, and the impressive Bionnassay glacier (**3**). Rising in long loops the way passes the

CHALET-REFUGE DU FIOUX (1520m, 2¾hrs) accommodation, refreshments; 24 beds; open end of May to end Sept (Tel 04 50 93 52 43).

About 10mins later you arrive on the **Col de Voza** (1653m, 3hrs, *refreshments, water supply, wc*). This gentle saddle is crossed by the Tramway du Mont Blanc (**2**), an electrified rack railway that climbs from St Gervais-les-Bains to the Nid d'Aigle. There's a halt here, and a bar-restaurant beside the line. The alternative TMB route from Les Contamines comes from the track on the right to join the main route to Les Houches. The large hotel building is the **Village de Vacances APAS** which has 150 places and is open from mid-June to mid-Sept (Tel 04 50

54 44 65). For the descent to Les Houches cross the railway and turn left along a rising track, then branch right when it forks.

The left branch continues to rise for about 30mins to

HOTEL LE PRARION, located at an altitude of 1860m with magnificent views. The hotel is open from June to early Sept, has 15 *dortoir* places and 19 beds (Tel 04 50 54 40 07; yves@prarion.com).

The Chamonix aiguilles, seen from the TMB below Col de Voza, spread in a line above the Vallée de l'Arve

The graceful line of the Chamonix aiguilles is on show as you wander along the track, as is the Vallée de l'Arve and the sprawl of Chamonix below. But then, as you descend the way becomes blinkered for a while by a border of trees. Winding downhill, and passing several ski tows, come to the two buildings of La Tuile (1370m), one of which is a restaurant, where the track makes a hairpin, and a few minutes later come to the lower station of the Télésiège de Maison-Neuve. Here the track becomes a metalled road, and in another 10mins there's a junction on a bend. Turn right.

Having left the main descending road, the way now crosses a bridge over the Nant Jorland stream, and about

1min later, when the road forks, keep ahead (the left branch) along a no-through road. This curves by houses and becomes a track which you follow all the way downhill to **Les Houches (1)**. When you come to the main road opposite Hotel Slalom, turn right, soon passing the valley station of the Bellevue cableway, and come to the heart of the village by the tourist office.

LES HOUCHES (1007m, 4½hrs) Office de tourisme (Tel 04 50 55 50 62; info@leshouches.com; **www.leshouches.com**); hotels, gîte, camping; shops, restaurants, banks, ATM, PTT, railway, buses, téléphèrique. Lower-priced accommodation: Chalet-Refuge Michel Fagot in the centre of the village, 36 dortoir places, open mid-Dec to end of Sept (Tel 04 50 54 42 28; reservation@gite-fagot.com); Hotel Les Campanules, 120 beds, open end Dec to mid-Sept (Tel 04 50 54 40 71; hotel-campanules@wanadoo.fr). For a full list of hotels, contact the tourist office.

For walkers tackling the TMB by the traditional anti-clockwise route, Les Houches is the starting point. The heart of the village has a lively buzz to it in summer, with new arrivals gathering there with a mixture of anticipation and apprehension prior to setting out for their first col. Having already walked the lion's share of the route, you may earn a few 'Brownie points' as newcomers quiz you about conditions on some of the passes. But don't feel too smug – there are some tough days still to come! One of the toughest of them all must be faced tomorrow.

ALTERNATIVE STAGE 7

Les Contamines – Refuge de Miage – Les Houches

Start point	Les Contamines (1167m)
Distance	18km
Height gain	1318m
Height loss	1478m
Time	5–5½hrs
High point	Col de Tricot (2120m)
Transport options	Cableway (Bellevue – Les Houches)
	Cableway (Prarion – Les Houches/Les Chavants)
Accommodation	Truc (1¼hrs) – auberge
	Chalets de Miage (1½hrs) – refuge
	Col de Voza (4–4½hrs) – hotel
	Les Houches – hotels, dortoirs, gîte, camping

Of the two suggested routes to Les Houches this is the more challenging, but after some of the previous stages you should be mountain-fit by now, and this helter-skelter option should not cause too much trouble. It is a helter-skelter route too, with a steady climb to the Mont Truc ridge, followed by descent into the Miage glen; then a steep climb to Col de Tricot, after which a fairly steep descent leads to a crossing below the Bionnassay glacier on a Himalayan-style suspension bridge. Yet another climb follows, leading up to the Bellevue ridge before starting the final descent to Col de Voza and Les Houches. But all the expenditure of effort is worthwhile, for it's a scenic stage, a true 'high route' alternative to the standard TMB.

The walk begins beside the attractive 18th-century church in the centre of Les Contamines, where the Chemin du P'tou rises along its left-hand side. Maintain direction at crossroads, but at the third of these, almost opposite Hotel Clef des Champs, turn left then right into the continuing Chemin du P'tou, which forks after a few paces. Take the left branch, a broad stony track rising to yet another crossing road. Continue directly ahead, and when you return to the road, bear left then right between

See Stage 7 for route map.

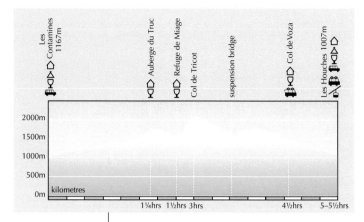

old farm buildings to reach a car park at **La Frasse** (1263m, 10mins) with public toilets and drinking water.

Entering the Réserve Naturelle Contamines-Montjoie walk up the Chemin des Granges, which soon becomes a track/dirt road that actually winds all the way to the Chalets du Truc – although the TMB takes a recommended footpath alternative. This begins about 25mins above La Frasse, where a signpost indicates a path on the right (1512m) – destination Le Truc. When it forks after a few paces take the left-hand upper path, which climbs quite steeply in places and has exposed tree roots demanding attention. After another 20–25mins or so rejoin the track, turn right and follow this to the

> **AUBERGE DU TRUC** (1720m, 1¼hrs) accommodation, refreshments; 28 dortoir places; open mid-June to mid-Sept (Tel 04 50 93 12 48).

The auberge stands in an open meadow with a fine view of the Dômes de Miage and their glaciers to the southeast, while in the opposite direction the view extends down through the Val Montjoie **(4)** to its confluence with the lower Vallée de l'Arve. A short walk north of the auberge leads to the rounded summit of Mont Truc (1811m) for a greater panoramic view.

The TMB passes alongside the auberge, swings round the meadowland and forks 4mins later. Take the right branch and descend a lightly wooded hillside into the Vallon de Miage, a typical U-shaped glacier-carved valley occupied by the Chalets de Miage. Come onto a track at the foot of the slope, turn right and, having crossed a bridge, take a path on the left which leads directly to the

REFUGE DE MIAGE (1559m, 1½hrs) accommodation, refreshments; 37 dortoir places, 2 beds; open June to mid-Sept (Tel 04 50 93 22 91).

On the north side of the valley above the refuge, Col de Tricot can be clearly seen. It's a sobering view, for in one glance it's possible to absorb almost 600m of ascent required to gain it. The path tacks its way to and fro and appears formidable. But the TMB has tackled tougher ascents than this, so don't lose heart as you leave the refuge on the continuing path that cuts a way through meadows towards the foot of the Tricot slope. Take the right branch at a fork, and 3mins later break off to the left, now rising northeast in numerous zigzags to gain the grassy **Col de Tricot** (2120m, 3hrs) about 1½hrs after leaving the Chalets de Miage. The view from the col is not as wide-ranging as you may have wished, but on the descent to a crossing of the torrent below the Glacier de Bionnassay **(3)** new mountains and glaciers are revealed from behind intruding spurs.

Grass slopes lead down the north side of the ridge crossed at the col, and before long the path scuffs among clumps of alpenrose whilst gaining a view of the Aiguilles de Bionnassay and du Goûter with the cascading Bionnassay glacier adding its character to the landscape. On the hillside ahead you should also be able to make out the track of the Tramway du Mont Blanc **(2)**, which will be crossed at Col de Voza.

Descending steeply among trees the path brings you below the rubble-strewn snout of the glacier. On coming to a path junction ignore the left branch which goes to Bionnassay, and continue down to a Himalayan-style suspension bridge across the frantic, discoloured glacial

Both the Aiguille and Glacier de Bionnassay are on show from the trail below Col de Tricot

torrent (c1650m). A variety of bridges have been built to carry TMB walkers across this torrent in the past, but each one has succumbed to either avalanche or flood. Hopefully this will last a little longer than some of its predecessors.

Once across, the way scrambles over rocks and enters woodland that clothes the right-hand lateral moraine of the retreating glacier. Now the path goes up the moraine crest and emerges to an open meadow with excellent views. At a T-junction of paths turn left and, contouring, pass through a gate to another path junction. Once again the left-hand option descends to Bionnassay, while the TMB route (signed Col de Voza) rises through a second gate and becomes an undulating path across a steep but partially wooded slope. Emerging from the trees, walk across an open meadow towards the line of the Tramway du Mont Blanc and a first view into the Vallée de l'Arve (the Chamonix valley).

Walk down a broad path to pass alongside the refurbished Hotel Bellevue (1786m), and 10mins later arrive on the **Col de Voza** (1653m, 4–4½hrs, *refreshments*). It is here that you join the main TMB route described in Stage 7, to which you should refer for details of the continuing descent to Les Houches **(1)**.

STAGE 8
Les Houches – Le Brévent – La Flégère

Start point	Les Houches (1007m)
Distance	17km
Height gain	1546m
Height loss	772m
Time	6–6½hrs
High point	Le Brévent (2526m)
Transport options	Bus (Les Houches – Chamonix)
	Cablecar (Chamonix – Le Brévent)
	Bus (Chamonix – Les Praz de Chamonix)
	Cablecar (Les Praz – La Flégère)
Accommodation	Bellachat (3–3½hrs) – refuge
	La Flégère – refuge

The steep and seemingly never-ending ascent of Le Brévent from the valley bed below Les Houches makes this one of the toughest stages of all. However, once out of the thick forest cover of the lower slopes, the path looks directly across the valley to Mont Blanc and the Bossons glacier, providing every possible excuse to pause frequently in order to enjoy that wonderful snowy vista. For more than two centuries Le Brévent itself has been recognised as one of the greatest of all viewpoints from which to study Mont Blanc and, given favourable conditions, will surely be one of the highlights of your tour.

If the view from Le Brévent is exciting, so too is the panorama from the refuge at La Flégère, where one gazes southeast along the highway of the Mer de Glace to the Grandes Jorasses – last seen from above Courmayeur. But much of the walk is of the highest scenic quality – so pray for good weather and clear visibility, and enjoy the challenge.

Finally, before leaving Les Houches, consider your plans for Stage 9. Should you anticipate spending an overnight at Refuge Les Grands, you'll need to carry food, as it's a self-catering only refuge. Les Houches is the last opportunity to buy supplies.

From the tourist office in the centre of Les Houches walk along the main street in the direction of Chamonix, then turn left down the road signed to St-Gervais and

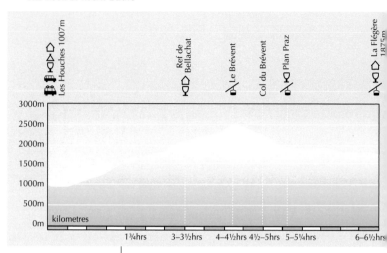

Les Houches 1007m
Ref de Bellachat
Le Brévent
Col du Brévent
Plan Praz
La Flégère 1877m

3000m
2500m
2000m
1500m
1000m
500m
0m   kilometres

1¾hrs   3–3½hrs   4–4½hrs 4½–5hrs 5–5¼hrs   6–6½hrs

Sallanches. Cross a bridge over a major road, turn right to cross the railway, and immediately right again into the Chemin des Eaux Rousses at 990m. After passing houses enter forest where the way forks. Take the upper branch, a track which forks again. Once more take the upper branch, and again when it forks take the left-hand option.

Rising through forest in zigzags, after about 25mins from Les Houches come to a junction and bear left, climbing still on a route signed to Christ Roi. About 15mins later reach a crossing track above a lone house.

For the TMB turn right and 3mins later you arrive at the base of the towering concrete statue of **Le Christ Roi (30)** ('Christ the King'; 1196m, 45mins). The stony track slants uphill above a stone building, and in a further 6mins you come to yet another junction. Continue ahead, and after a longish contour section take the upper left-hand path at the next junction. This brings you onto a road, where you turn right to reach a car park for the Parc Merlet mountain zoo **(29)**. After the first section of car park take a path cutting above the road, now entering the Réserve Naturelle Carlaveyron. At future junctions follow signs for Bellachat or Brévent.

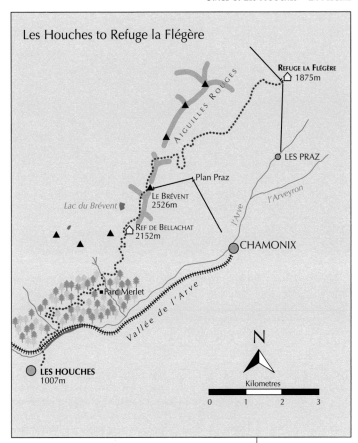

Eventually come out of forest above the zoo where the path dips into a narrow gully, the Vouillards ravine, which has a stream flowing through it. Climbing out of this ravine involves using metal steps and handrails for security, then the route continues along a slightly exposed section from which to enjoy uninterrupted views of Mont Blanc. Rising again, in and out of patches of forest then across open hillsides, you gain height steeply on

Almost every step of the way between Le Brévent and Refuge de Bellachat enjoys a huge panorama

occasion, until at last, by another path junction and with incredible views, you arrive at the small timber-built

REFUGE DE BELLACHAT (2152m, 3–3½hrs) accommodation, refreshments; 28 dortoir places; open late June to mid-Sept (Tel 04 50 53 43 23).

The path climbs on above the refuge, and 5mins later you branch right when it forks. About 10mins later Le Brévent comes into view. Twisting up onto a ridge you gain yet more tantalising views across the valley, then wander through a rocky landscape before making a last twisting ascent to a shoulder just below the summit. To visit the summit crown of Le Brévent from here takes only 5mins and is a diversion worth making. The path on the right goes directly to it.

Le Brévent (27) (2526m, 4–4½hrs, *refreshments*) provides a wonderful grandstand from which to study Mont Blanc across the way, and also an aerial perspective of Chamonix **(28)**, sprawling almost 1500 vertical metres below. There's a café-bar on the summit terrace, and

The well-made TMB path below the summit of Le Brévent

another restaurant at the head of the cableway just below the top.

Return to the path junction at the shoulder and turn right on a track/ski piste sloping downhill. A few minutes later come to a small col on the right. A direct descent can be made to Plan Praz via that col on a ski piste, but the recommended TMB route keeps left, now on a path, towards Col du Brévent. This way becomes rough, steep and rocky in places. Two steel ladders and metal handrails for security aid the descent of one particularly steep place, below which you enter a hollow then weave a route through a boulder wilderness guided by standard waymarks, cairns and red painted spots. So reach **Col du Brévent** (2368m) about 30mins after leaving the summit.

The long-distance GR5 (La Grande Traversée des Alpes) **(26)**, whose route has been shared since Col de la Croix du Bonhomme on Stage 6, now parts from the TMB by cutting left towards Col d'Anterne. The TMB, however, continues ahead and is soon twisting steeply down, but then easing on the approach to the ski-scarred Plan Praz, about 30mins from the col.

On coming to the cableway building of La Parsa, take the path heading left away from Plan Praz. About 15mins later come to a three-way junction and take the middle option ahead, where a pleasant path makes a descending traverse across the slopes of Montagne de la Parsa. This leads to a crossing track, where you walk directly ahead on a continuing path which cuts round the hillside, then against cliffs before resuming among shrubs. One or two further junctions are met here in close succession, and on each occasion you simply follow signs for La Flégère.

Now in the open grasslands of **Charlanon** (1812m) cross the track once more to twist up the hillside among trees and shrubs, then cross a spur from which La Flégère can be seen. There follows a delightful contour where the path curves round a series of hillside bays, in one of which you cut through an avalanche protection wall. At the end of the final bay (or combe) climb a short but steep and rocky section eased with steps and handrails, and before long reach the Flégère cablecar station and, just below it,

REFUGE LA FLÉGÈRE (1875m, 6–6½hrs) accommodation, refreshments; 66 dortoir places, 21 beds; open mid-June to mid-Sept (Tel 06 03 58 28 14; bellay.catherine@wanadoo.fr).

Despite the barren nature of the ski-scarred landscape immediately behind, and the presence of the cablecar station nearby, the refuge is an idyllic place to spend a night. From the terrace, and from the dining room windows, the view across the valley is exquisite. Panning from Col de Balme to Col de Voza the panorama encompasses all the Chamonix aiguilles and a succession of glaciers, the most impressive of which is the Mer de Glace (25) which acts as a highway of ice leading to the big wall of the Grandes Jorasses. Although Mont Blanc can be seen from here it is perhaps less impressive from this angle than some of its neighbours, but all in all the scene is truly memorable – especially when lit by the evening sun.

STAGE 9
La Flégère – Col de Balme – Trient

Start point	La Flégère (1875m)
Distance	19km
Height gain	1217m (or 1368m)
Height loss	1802m (or 1953m)
Time	7½hrs
High point	Aiguillette des Posettes (2201m) (or Lac Blanc (2352m) on optional route)
Transport options	Cablecar (La Flégère – Les Praz)
	Bus (Les Praz – Col des Montets)
Accommodation	Tré-le-Champ (2½hrs) – auberge/gîte
	Col de Balme (5½–6hrs) – refuge
	Le Peuty (7–7¼hrs) – gîte, camping
	Trient – dortoirs
	Les Grands (6¾–7¼hrs) – CAS refuge (Les Grands *variante*)
Alternative routes	La Flégère – Lac Blanc – Col des Montets (see below)
	Col de Balme – Refuge les Grands (see below)

Of the alternative options available, a visit to Lac Blanc rates highly. Understandably popular as it is, Lac Blanc is such an idyllic location that it deserves to be on the list of 'must visit' sites for walkers in the area. However, to add this to the main day's route as described would be too much for most TMB walkers, so an overnight at Tré-le-Champ is advised.

The other alternative, to Refuge Les Grands, only departs from the main route at Col de Balme, and is offered for self-contained walkers aiming to take the Fenêtre d'Arpette *variante* on the way to Champex tomorrow. The refuge is infrequently manned, and even when it is, no food is available. Only stay there if you are carrying supplies – the refuge has self-catering facilities.

Two final warnings before setting out. Part of the main descent route from Tête aux Vents is **extremely steep**, and has a series of near-vertical ladders, rungs, platforms and steps to help negotiate a route down rock slabs. This is the steepest section of the whole TMB, and is not recommended for anyone with a tendency towards vertigo – an alternative is offered. The climb as described to Col de Balme goes along **an exposed ridge** by the Aiguillette des Posettes – if there is any chance of a storm, this should be avoided and an obvious lower route taken from Le Tour (not described).

Main TMB Route to Tré-Le-Champ

Out of the refuge turn left and descend to a track which curves to the left and 3mins later brings you to a junction. Go straight ahead for another 3mins to a second junction near a skiers' bar-restaurant, La Chavanne (closed in summer). Walk ahead alongside the building onto a narrow path that makes a steady rising traverse across the hillside.

About 45mins from La Flégère come to an attractive waterfall spraying through a gully in the left-hand cliff face. This waterfall is the overflow from Lac Blanc, and the path crosses the stream below it before the stream spills in more cascades down the grassy hillside. In another 6mins come to a path junction at the **Chalet des Chéserys** (2005m, 50–55mins). Ignoring options to right and left continue ahead, rising more steeply now and gaining height with zigzags to reach a prominent cairn. Beyond this, climb on for a few more minutes to gain the high point of the **Tête aux Vents** (2132m, 1hr 10mins) marked by a large boundary cairn at a four-way junction

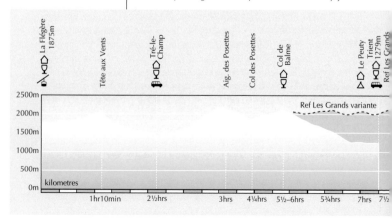

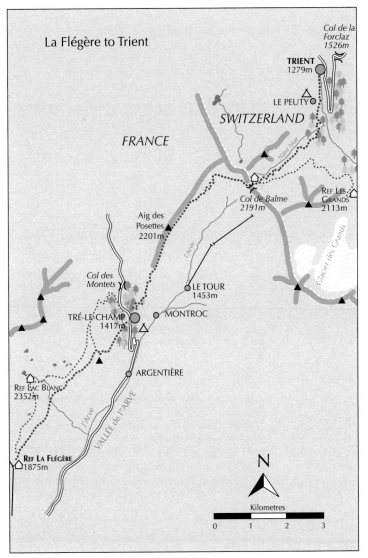

La Flégère to Trient

of paths. This is a boundary of the Réserve Naturelle des Aiguilles Rouges (24) that was founded in 1974.

The right-hand path carries the main TMB steeply down to Tré-le-Champ via the ladders mentioned in the introduction to this stage. Anyone nervous about this route should take the *variante* described below.

TMB VARIANTE: TÊTE AUX VENTS – COL DES MONTETS

Take the path ahead, signed to Col des Montets and with direct views of the Aiguilles Rouges, and soon come to another junction where the left-hand path visits the Lacs des Chéserys and Lac Blanc. Ignore this option, continue ahead and, without deviating from the trail, follow the Grand Balcon Sud along the slopes of the Aiguilles Rouges until the descent to Col des Montets begins in earnest with numerous zigzags tackling the steep vegetated hillside. It's unnecessary to go all the way to Col des Montets, so take the right branch when the path forks, and this will bring you to the road on the south side of the col at 1430m. Walk down this a short way to find the main TMB path on the left-hand side signed Col de Balme and Aiguillette des Posettes (about 1½hrs from Tête aux Vents).

Main TMB Route to Tré-Le-Champ

Turning right at the boundary cairn, the path is steep from the outset and descends in zigzags with an airy bird's-eye view onto the rooftops of Argentière 800m below. Before long come to the first of the metal rungs and ladders that enable non-climbers to tackle the slabs. Although it's a sensational descent, the route should be perfectly safe, but you must take care to avoid dislodging stones onto anyone below. At the foot of the first series of aids the path angles left and makes a few zigzags before coming to another succession of ladders, rungs and timber-braced steps. Just below, climbers may be seen in action on the Aiguillette d'Argentière, and the path tucks behind this pinnacle when the last of the aids has been descended.

In a little under 2hrs from La Flégère, shortly after reaching the treeline, the path forks. One branch goes ahead to Argentière, while the TMB swings left for the continuing descent to Tré-le-Champ among trees and

This small wayside tarn above La Flégère reflects some of the glories of the Mont Blanc range

OPTIONAL ROUTE VIA LAC BLANC

There are two ways of reaching Lac Blanc from La Flégère: via the chairlift to l'Index, where an easy and very popular path contours to the right in order to reach the lake and its refuge, or by the path described below, in 1½hrs.

From the terrace at La Flégère turn left and descend to a track curving round to the left. About 3mins later come to a junction where you continue straight ahead, reaching a second junction in another 3mins. This is by the bar-restaurant La Chavanne (closed in summer), where you turn left. Before long the stony track breaks into more amenable paths as you gain height. In a little under 30mins pass above an unnamed pool and, continuing to climb, another 35mins will bring you to the junction with a path from Les Chéserys. About 6mins above this join the route from l'Index for the final 10min walk to **Lac Blanc** (2352m, 1½hrs). Beside the lake stands **Refuge Lac Blanc** (accommodation, refreshments; 40 dortoir places, manned from mid-June to end Sept; Tel 04 50 53 49 14). The situation is magnificent, and at least an hour should be devoted to making a circuit of the lake and simply absorbing the views.

To rejoin the TMB take the signed path which heads northeast (left when descending from the lake) towards the Lacs des Chéserys, soon descending a metal ladder that tackles an outcrop, then on to a solitary lake. Beyond this the clear path descends to the right of the Chéserys lakes and comes to a junction by a large boundary cairn. If you're not unnerved by prospects of more near-vertical ladders, turn right to a second large cairn (Tête aux Vents), where you turn left on the main TMB route described above. However, if you would rather avoid these aids, bear left and follow the path as described above to Col des Montets.

shrubs. In 2¼hrs the path spills out onto the Col des Montets–Chamonix road. For the continuing TMB to Col de Balme, cross the road and turn left (see details below). For accommodation or refreshments cross the road to a track angling down to the right where, very shortly, you enter the hamlet of

TRÉ-LE-CHAMP (1417m, 2½hrs) accommodation, refreshments at Auberge la Boerne; 32 dortoir places; open all year (Tel 04 50 54 05 14; contact@la-boerne.fr; **www.la-boerne.fr**).

Main TMB Route to Col de Balme

Coming onto the road above Tré-le-Champ cross over and turn left to a pair of old stone houses and a small chapel. Just beyond these a path rises above the road, enters forest and shortly comes to a signpost directing the way to the right to Col de Balme and Aiguillette des Posettes. There follows a lengthy climb through forest in numerous zig-zags. Keep left at junctions and emerge above the treeline about 45mins from the road to views that improve in quality and extent the higher you go up the Posettes arête.

The path maintains a regular gradient, rising in a further series of zigzags among alpenrose, juniper and bilberry shrubs. About 1¾hrs from the road the path forks once more at 2130m. The right branch descends to Le Tour while the TMB continues up to the crown of **L'Aiguillette des Posettes** (2201m, 4hrs), which is marked by a modest cairn. The panorama is another highlight of the tour, for not only does it encompass the Chamonix aiguilles and Mont Blanc, but includes the rusty chain of the Aiguilles Rouges, and the large rock-cradled Emosson lake in the northwest.

Over the summit the path unravels into several braid-ings as you descend past the top of a ski tow to the grassy saddle of **Col des Posettes** (1997m), where a signpost stands at a multi-way junction. Take the right-hand track marked to Col de Balme, and when it forks 2mins later take the left branch. Just 1min after this leave the track for a path climbing left to loop up the hillside, passing beneath another ski tow and beyond avalanche fences to yet another path junction. Turn right and contour the hillside on the final approach to Col de Balme **(23)** and the

REFUGE DU COL DE BALME (2191m, 5½–6hrs) accommodation, refreshments; 26 dortoir places (Tel 04 50 54 02 33).

TMB VARIANTE: COL DE BALME – REFUGE LES GRANDS

On leaving the refuge on Col de Balme bear right to a footpath junction, then take the left branch signed to Les Grands, Chalet du Glacier and Col de la Forclaz. Reluctant to lose much height, this path contours for about 5mins, then descends a little, sometimes crossing patches of snow even in mid-summer. In places it is a narrow path, but, always clearly defined, it provides views down to Trient and across to Col de la Forclaz.

Having crossed a rocky section, about 40mins from the col the path turns a spur with the upper Vallée du Trient **(21)** now seen ahead, with the ridge broken by the Fenêtre d'Arpette on the far side. Undulating along the hillside among alpenroses, the way climbs again to a view of the Glacier du Trient ahead and, above to the right, the smaller Glacier des Grands. The highest point is reached at about 2150m, immediately before descending directly to the

REFUGE LES GRANDS (2113m, 7–7¼hrs) self-catering accommodation only; 15 dortoir places, cooking facilities, water supply, infrequently wardened; open mid-June to mid-Oct (for reservations Tel 026 660 65 04).

If the refuge is not crowded a night spent here can be very pleasant. The hut faces across the valley, but the Pointe d'Orny, which guards the upper *firn* Plateau du Trient above the Trient glacier's icefall, is clearly seen. The route to the Fenêtre d'Arpette is also on show, its bold loops climbing the opposite hillside, while above the refuge to the south hangs the rippled Glacier des Grands. The hut was only opened in the 1990s, and although meals are not available, cooking facilities are adequate, and there's a good supply of crockery and cutlery.

Note Should you decide to continue down to Le Peuty, Trient or even Col de la Forclaz for accommodation, refer to Alternative Stage 10 below for details.

Standing on the Franco-Swiss border, and with a celebrated view along the Vallée de l'Arve, the TMB path once again divides. The standard route descends directly to Le Peuty and Trient in the Vallée du Trient **(21)**, while a *variante* (see box above) angles round to the small, mostly unmanned Refuge les Grands for suitably equipped trekkers planning to cross the Fenêtre d'Arpette tomorrow.

For Le Peuty and Trient, go out of the refuge, bear left for a few paces to a signpost directing the descent path down into the Vallon de Nant Noir. At first the path goes down in long loops, but once you enter forest the way steepens with tighter zigzags, emerging to a rough pastureland in the Vallée du Trient. Bear left, cross the Nant Noir stream and wander down to the hamlet of

LE PEUTY (1328m, 7–7½hrs) accommodation at the gîte, Refuge Du Peuty; 37 dortoir places; open mid-June to mid-Sept (Tel 027 722 09 38); camping nearby.

Continue down the road for a further 10mins to enter

TRIENT (1279m, 7–7¾hrs) refreshments, food store, accommodation at: Auberge Mont Blanc, 60 dortoir places, 20 beds, open all year (Tel 027 767 15 05; info@aubergemontblanc.com); La Grande Ourse, 38 dortoir places, 18 beds, plus apartments, open all year (Tel 027 722 17 54; **www.la-grande-ourse.ch**).

This small village nestles on a slope of meadowland below Col de la Forclaz, whose road fortunately bypasses it. The Glacier du Trient is clearly seen at the head of the narrow valley it has created, acting as a lure to the many walkers and trekkers who congregate there most days in summer, for the village is not only on the route of the TMB, but is also used as a staging post on the classic Chamonix to Zermatt Walkers' Haute Route.

STAGE 10
Trient – Alp Bovine – Champex

Start point	Trient (1279m)
Distance	17km
Height gain	929m
Height loss	742m
Time	5½hrs
High point	Collet Portalo (2040m)
Accommodation	Col de la Forclaz (45mins) – hotel/dortoir, camping
	Bovine (2½hrs) – emergency dortoir only
	Champex d'en Haut (4½hrs) – gîte, hotel
	Champex – hotels, pensions, gîte, camping
Alternative route	Les Grands – Fenêtre d'Arpette – Champex (see Alternative Stage 10)

Of the two routes to Champex, this is the easier – but it does have its challenging sections, and some surprising views of the Rhône Valley, Bernese Alps and Grand Combin. For the Fenêtre d'Arpette *variante*, see below.

The day begins by walking up the hillside to the Col de la Forclaz, and to achieve this you make your way above the church in Trient to the main road, where you bear right. A short distance along this, turn off by a stone cross on a broad grass track rising above the road. Entering woodland, this track brings you onto the Forclaz road. Bear right for a few paces, then cross a footbridge to a continuing trail which climbs steeply, eventually bringing you onto a lovely level footpath beside a *bisse* (irrigation channel). Turn left, shortly to arrive at the

COL DE LA FORCLAZ (19) (1526m, 45mins) refreshments, shop, bus to Martigny, accommodation in Hotel du Col de la Forclaz; 40 dortoir places, 35 beds, camping, open mid-Dec to Nov (Tel 027 722 26 88; colforclazhotel@bluewin.ch; **www.coldelaforclaz.ch**).

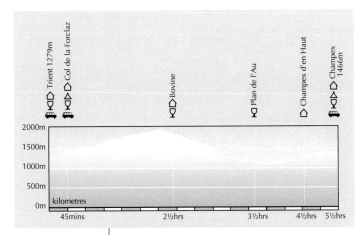

For the TMB, take the path immediately over the col which goes alongside a building and edges a meadow before entering woodland. Twisting among trees the path gains height steeply in places with views into the Rhône valley, and works its way round the Combe des Faces to a junction of paths (1725m, 1½hrs), where the left-hand option descends to La Caffe and La Croix. Ignore this turning and continue ahead, still rising in woodland for another 30mins, before passing to the left of a group of alp buildings (La Giète, 1884m) in an open basin. Beyond these buildings the way resumes among larch- and pine-woods, and, shortly after a welcome contour section where views are gained onto Martigny, the trail rises to the woodland edge and the high point known as **Collet Portalo** (2040m, 2hrs 20mins). From here the Bovine alp buildings can be seen a short distance ahead and on a clear day, the distant snowy mass of the Grand Combin.

ALP BOVINE (1987m, 2½hrs) emergency dortoir accommodation, refreshments.

Nestling on a gentle slope of pastureland facing northeast along the Rhône valley, Alp Bovine provides a contrast

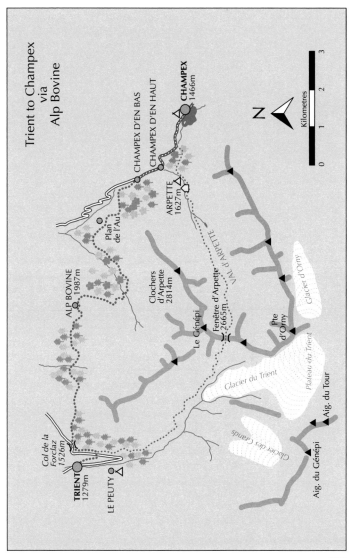

Trient to Champex
via
Alp Bovine

CHAMPEX D'EN BAS
CHAMPEX D'EN HAUT
CHAMPEX
1466m

ARPETTE
1627m

Plan
de l'Au

ALP BOVINE
1987m

Clochers
d'Arpette
2814m

Le Génépi

Fenêtre d'Arpette
2665m

VAL D'ARPETTE

Pte
d'Orny

Glacier d'Orny

Plateau du Trient

Glacier du Trient

Col de la
Forclaz
1526m

TRIENT
1279m

LE PEUTY

Glacier des Grands

Aig. du Tour

Aig. du Génépi

N

0   1   2   3
Kilometres

between the simple pastoral life of the traditional alp herdsman and farmer and the modern high-tech agriculturalist whose orchards and vineyards pattern the valley and hillsides 1500m below. Whilst remaining in essence a working dairy farm, thanks to passing walkers the farmer's income is supplemented by the sale of refreshments. Simple dortoir accommodation may be available here.

Beyond the alp the original TMB path makes an eastbound contour, then curves sharply south along the hillside, crosses a stream and descends steeply into the wooded Vallon de Six-Fours. The rocky path crosses a series of streams before descending a more open slope and coming at last onto a track contouring to the right. Bear right and follow this round the hillside to the farm buildings of **Plan de l'Au** (1330m, 3½hrs, *refreshments*), where the track becomes a narrow metalled road. Just 2mins beyond the farm break off to the right on a footpath rising to more woodland.

When the woodland path forks take the left branch, soon passing below a group of chalets and coming to a road at **Champex d'en Bas** (1340m, 4hrs 10mins). Turn right, pass the houses of this strung-out hamlet, and on reaching a minor crossroads at the upper end continue straight ahead to

CHAMPEX D'EN HAUT (1440m, 4½hrs) accommodation: auberge-gîte, Chalet Bon-Abri, 33 dortoir places, 42 beds, open all year (Tel 027 783 14 23; contact@gite-bonabri.com; **www.gite-bonabri. com**); Hotel-Club Sunways, 77 beds, open Dec to April and June to Sept (Tel 027 783 11 22).

About 300m beyond the Sunways hotel join the main valley road and turn right, rising to its highest point, then, sloping downhill and passing the La Breya chairlift, come to **Champex (18)** and the completion of your Tour.

CHAMPEX (1466m, 5½hrs) hotels, pensions, gîte, camping; restaurants, shops, PTT. Tourist information (Tel 027 783 12 27, champexlac@v-sb.ch; **www.**

lafouly.ch). Lower-priced accommodation: Pension En Plein Air, 48 dortoir places, 25 beds, open all year (Tel 027 783 23 50; pensionenpleinair@bluewin. ch); Au Club Alpin, 25 dortoir places, open all year (Tel 027 783 11 61); Chalet du Jardin Alpin, 8 dortoir places, 13 beds, self-catering only, open May to end-Oct (Tel 027 783 12 17, fondation.aubert@ bluewin.ch); Camping Les Rocailles, open all year (Tel 027 783 19 79) is located at the top end of the village.

Also known as Champex-Lac to emphasise its lakeside position, this neat little resort is a good place in which to celebrate completion of the walk and contemplate the highlights of the circuit, of which there will be many. So, congratulations to you and those who have walked the TMB with you. May your memories outweigh even your expectations of the route, and lead to many more great days in the Alps. ▸

The main route of the TMB via Alp Bovine gains a distant view of the Dents du Midi from just outside Champex

Buses depart Champex for Orsières, the railhead for the St Bernard Express which runs downvalley to Martigny and mainline services for Geneva.

ALTERNATIVE STAGE 10
Refuge Les Grands – Fenêtre d'Arpette – Champex

Start point	Refuge Les Grands (2113m)
Distance	13km
Height gain	1082m
Height loss	1729m
Time	6–6½ hrs
High point	Fenêtre d'Arpette (2665m)
Accommodation	Arpette (5–5½hrs) – hotel/dortoir, camping
	Champex – hotels, pensions, gîte, camping
Alternative route	Trient/Col de la Forclaz – Alp Bovine – Champex (see Stage 10)

Along with the Col des Fours *variante* on Stage 5, the Fenêtre d'Arpette is the highest pass on the TMB, and its crossing is at once challenging and scenically rewarding, whether approached from the west, as here, or from the east as on the standard anti-clockwise TMB. And tackling it on the final stage of the circuit ensures that you finish on a high note. It must be stressed, however, that you should not attempt this route early in the season when snow may be lying below the pass (you should be able to see this from Refuge Les Grands), or if a storm is forecast. Good weather and stable conditions underfoot are prerequisites for this stage. Should conditions not be favourable, divert to Col de la Forclaz from Chalet du Glacier below Les Grands, and follow the TMB route described as Stage 10 via Alp Bovine.

Take the descending path below Refuge Les Grands which soon slants diagonally along a shelf against a rock face, where a fixed cable gives reassurance. Once across this, zigzag steeply downhill along the left side of the little Vallon des Grands, passing a couple of small ruins and then entering pinewoods. Ignore the right-hand option where the path forks, and continue ahead until you reach the foot of the slope and another path junction by a footbridge spanning the milky torrent rushing from the Glacier du Trient. The continuing path goes to Le Peuty (in 30mins) and Trient (45mins), but for the Fenêtre d'Arpette and

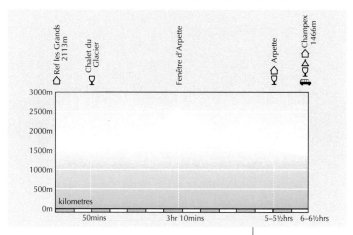

Champex cross the bridge to another path junction by the **Chalet du Glacier** (1583m, 50mins, *refreshments*). ▶

Turn right for the Fenêtre, and a few paces beyond the Chalet take the left fork; 10mins later the path forks again and once more you take the left branch. The way is deceptively undemanding at first, angling across the hillside and passing through a few stands of trees and shrubs to views of the glacier ahead, but then the gradient steepens above the low ruins of Vésevey (2096m) and, when you look back to the north, long views show ridge upon ridge of distant mountains. Just below the ridge crest waymarks lead across a jumble of rocks and boulders, and suddenly you arrive at the **Fenêtre d'Arpette** (2665m, 3hrs 10mins), a rocky gateway or a window on a new world.

The Fenêtre is a classic mountain pass and a profound divide. On the west side the glacier responsible for carving the narrow Vallée du Trient is still very much in evidence despite advanced recession, spilling from a gleaming *firn* plateau guarded by Pointe d'Orny and the Aiguille du Tour. On the east side, however, there is no sign of glacier. Instead vast sweeps of scree fan down into the Val d'Arpette **(20)**. In the distance shines the snow-capped Grand Combin. Relax here and enjoy the scene

If it looks unwise to tackle the Fenêtre, turn left here and follow the path alongside the Bisse du Trient **(22)** to Col de la Forclaz (45mins), where you can join the Bovine route described as Stage 10.

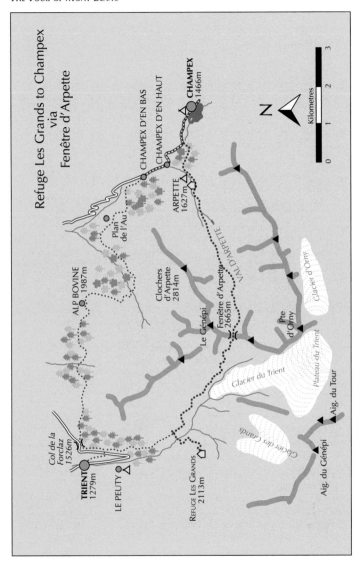

Refuge Les Grands to Champex
via
Fenêtre d'Arpette

TMB walkers relax on the rocky Fenêtre d'Arpette at 2665m

before tackling the descent to Champex, for this will prove almost as tiring as the ascent.

Caution is advised on the initial descent which is extremely steep, the path (or paths) being somewhat gritty and with snow patches often lying as late as mid-summer. These paths lead down into a rocky basin and a chaotic boulder tip, where waymarks and small cairns direct the way. Take care when negotiating these boulders, for some of the slabs tend to rock under your weight, and this is no place to fall.

Once across the boulder field the path is better defined as it leads down the left-hand side of the valley, exchanging boulders and scree for grass and shrubs and, eventually, trees. Once you reach the lower valley the path crosses and recrosses the stream several times before coming to open pastures and a track which passes a group of chalets and then draws level with the

RELAIS D'ARPETTE (1627m, 5–5½hrs) refreshments; 86 dortoir places, 14 beds, camping, open May to end of Oct (Tel 027 783 12 21; info@arpette.ch).

About 2mins past the hotel take a signed path on the left which descends in woodland to a *bisse* (an irrigation channel). Follow this through the woods, gaining snatched views over the valley in which lie Champex

The eastern view from the Fenêtre d'Arpette shows long scree fans that sweep into the Val d'Arpette

d'en Haut and Champex d'en Bas to the craggy peaks of the Dents du Midi. Eventually emerge from the woodland to pass beneath the La Breya chairlift by a small pond, then up a short slope to a crossing road. Turn left and join the main road, where you bear right and wander downhill into **Champex (18)**, which effectively marks the completion of your Tour of Mont Blanc. Now's the time to celebrate. Congratulations on having achieved a great walk!

CHAMPEX (1466m, 6–6½hrs) hotels, pensions, gîte, camping, restaurants, shops, PTT, bus to Orsières for trains to Martigny. Tourist information (Tel 027 783 12 27; champexlac@v-sb.ch; **www.lafouly.ch**). Lower-priced accommodation: Pension En Plein Air, 48 dortoir places, 25 beds, open all year (Tel 027 783 23 50; pensionenpleinair@bluewin.ch); Au Club Alpin, 25 dortoir places, open all year (Tel 027 783 11 61); Chalet du Jardin Alpin, 8 dortoir places, 13 beds, self-catering only; open May to end-Oct (Tel 027 783 12 17; fondation.aubert@bluewin.ch.

Camping Les Rocailles, open all year (Tel 027 783 19 79) is located at the top end of the village.

APPENDIX A
Accommodation

The following list details accommodation sources in sequential order when following the traditional counter-clockwise route. The number of places and type of accommodation on offer, and dates when open, are given where known. Further details may be obtained from the various tourist offices. Additions or alterations to the list would be welcomed by the author.

Please note: d = dortoir places b = beds pl = places (details unknown)

FRANCE

LES HOUCHES

Office de Tourisme, 74310 Les Houches (Tel 04 50 55 50 62, info@leshouches.com; www.leshouches.com)

Chalet-Refuge Michel Fagot, Allée des Sorbiers, BP22, 74310 Les Houches (Tel 04 50 54 42 28, reservation@gite-fagot.com; www.gite-fagot.com) – 36d: mid-Dec–end Sept

Gîte-Auberge le Crêt, 128 Route des Aillouds, 74310 Les Houches (Tel 04 50 55 52 27; aubergelecret@wanadoo.fr) – 10d, 7b: Dec–Oct

Hotel Les Campanules, 450 Route de Coupeau, 74310 Les Houches (Tel 04 50 54 40 71, hotel-campanules@wanadoo.fr; www.hotel-campanules.com) – 120b: end Dec–mid-Sept

Hotel le Prarion, 74170 Saint Gervais (Tel 04 50 54 40 07, yves@prarion.com; www.prarion.com) – 15d, 19b: mid-June–early Sept

Village de Vacances APAS, Col de Voza (Tel 04 50 54 44 65, voza@apas.asso.fr; http://www.chamonix.com/village-apas-btp,119-177301,en.html – 150pl: mid-June–mid-Aug

Hotel Bellevue, Col de Voza – 24b

Chalet-Refuge du Fioux, Route de Bionnassay, 74170 Saint Gervais (Tel 04 50 93 52 43; serge.botholier@neuf.fr) – 24b: end May–end Sept

Auberge de Bionnassay, 3084 Route de Bionnassay, 74170 Saint Gervais (Tel 04 50 93 45 23; www.auberge-bionnassay.com) – 20d, 18b: June–end Sept

Gîte du Champel, Le Champel, 74170 Saint Gervais (Tel 04 50 47 77 55, gite@champel.fr) – 8d, 34b: June–mid-Sept

Le Peclet, Le Champel, 74170 Saint Gervais (Tel 06 84 18 45 55, lepeclet@orange.fr, www.lepeclet.fr) 6b: June–Sept

Refuge de Miage, 74170 Saint Gervais (Tel 04 50 93 22 91) – 37d, 2b: June–mid-Sept

Auberge du Truc, Chemin du Truc, 74170 Saint Gervais (Tel 04 50 93 12 48, aubergedutruc@hotmail.fr) – 28d: mid-June–mid-Sept

LES CONTAMINES-MONTJOIE

Office de Tourism, 18 Route de Notre Dame de la Gorge, BP7, 74170 Les Contamines-Montjoie (Tel 04 50 47 01 58, info@lescontamines.com; www.lescontamines.com)

Refuge du CAF, 22 Route du Plan du Moulin, 74170 Les Contamines (Tel 04 50 47 00 88) – 28d: mid-June–mid-Sept

Chalet Bonaventure, 135 Chemin du Nivorin d'en Bas, 74170 Les Contamines (Tel 04 50 47 23 53, camille.bonaventure@wanadoo.fr) – 8d: mid-June–mid-Sept

Hotel Christiania, 593 Route de ND de la Gorge, 74170 Les Contamines (Tel 04 50 47 02 72, hotel-christiania@wanadoo.fr; www.lechristiania-hotel.com) – b

Chalet-Hotel La Chemenaz, Les Hameaux du Lay, 74170 Les Contamines-Montjoie (Tel 04 50 47 02 44 www.chemenaz.com) – 112b

Gîte du Pontet, 2485 Route de N.D. de la Gorge, 74170 Les Contamines (Tel 04 50 47 04 04, campingdupontet@wanadoo.fr) – 32d: June–Sept

Refuge Nant Borrant, Chemin du Col du Bonhomme, 74170 Les Contamines (Tel 04 50 47 03 57, refugenantborrant@free.fr) – 35d: mid-June–Sept

Refuge de la Balme, Route Col du Bonhomme, 74170 Les Contamines (Tel 04 50 47 03 54) – 36d, 14b: mid-June–mid-Sept

Refuge de la Croix du Bonhomme, 73270 Beaufort/Doron (Tel 04 79 07 05 28, refuge-bonhomme@free.fr) – 113d: mid-June–mid-Sept

LES CHAPIEUX

Auberge de la Nova, Les Chapieux, 73700 Bourg St Maurice (Tel 04 79 89 07 15, info@refugelanova.com, www.refugelanova.com) – 35d, 35b: May–Oct

Chambre de Soleil, Les Chapieux, 73700 Bourg St Maurice (Tel 04 79 31 22, lesoleildeschapieux@gmail.com, www.leschambresdusoleil-montblanc.com – 14b

Refuge des Mottets, Vallée des Glaciers, 73700 Bourg St Maurice (Tel 04 79 07 01 70, refuge@lesmottets.com, www.lesmottets.com) – 90d: mid-June–mid-Sept

ITALY

Rifugio Elisabetta, Val Veni, 11013 Courmayeur (Tel 01 65 84 40 80, info@rifugioelisabetta.com) – 53d, 20b: mid-June–mid-Sept

Cabane du Combal, Val Veni, 11013 Courmayeur (Tel 01 65 17 56 421, cabaneducombal@gmail.com, www.cabaneducombal.com) – 23d: June–Sept

Rifugio Maison Vieille, Col Chécrouit, 11013 Courmayeur (Tel 337 23 09 79, info@maisonvieille.com; www.maisonvieille.com) – 50d: mid-June–end Sept

Rifugio Le Randonneur, Pra Neyron-Chécrouit, 11013 Courmayeur (Tel 349 53 68 898, info@randonneurmb.com, www.randonneurmb.com) – 25d and b: mid-June–end Sept

Camping-Gîte La Sorgente, Peuterey, Val Veni, 11013 Courmayeur (Tel 01 65 86 90 89, info@campingsorgente.net) – 8d, 20b: June–mid-Sept

Rifugio Monte Bianco, Val Veni, 11013 Courmayeur (Tel 01 65 86 90 97) – 14d, 50b: mid-June–mid-Sept

COURMAYEUR

Ufficio del Turismo: AIAT Monte Bianco, Piazzale Monte Bianco 13, 11013 Courmayeur (Tel 01 65 84 20 60, courmayeur@turismo.vda.it; www.lovevda.it)

Pensione Venezia, Strada della Villette 2, 11013 Courmayeur (Tel 01 65 84 24 61) – 25b

Hotel Select, Strada Regionale 27, 11013 Courmayeur (Tel 01 65 84 66 61, select@courmayeurhotel.com; www.courmayeurhotel.com) – 32b: mid-June–mid-Sept

Hotel Edelweiss, Via Marconi 42, 11013 Courmayeur (Tel 01 65 84 15 90, info@albergoedelweiss.it) – 55b: end June–end Sept

Hotel Svizzero, Strada Statale 26, 11013 Courmayeur (Tel 01 65 84 81 70, info@hotelsvizzero.com; www.hotelsvizzero.com) – 38b: June–Sept

Hotel Crampon, Via Villette 8, 11013 Courmayeur (Tel 01 65 84 23 85, info@crampon.it, www.crampon.it) – 46b: July–mid-Sept

Rifugio Giorgio Bertone, Mont de la Saxe, 11013 Courmayeur (Tel 01 65 84 46 12, info@rifugiobertone.com; www.rifugiobertone.it) – 55d, 14b: mid-June–end Sept

Rifugio Bonatti, Malatra – Val Ferret, 11013 Courmayeur (Tel 01 65 18 55 523, rifugiobonatti@gmail.com; www.rifugiobonatti.it) – 85d: March–April; June–Sept

Hotel Lavachey, Val Ferret, 11013 Courmayeur (Tel 01 65 86 97 23, www.lavachey.com) – 21b: mid-June–mid-Sept

Chalet Val Ferret, Arnuva, Val Ferret, 11013 Courmayeur (Tel 01 65 84 49 59, info@chaletvalferret.com; www.chaletvalferret.com) – 14b: June–Sept

Rifugio Elena, Pré de Bard, Val Ferret, 11013 Courmayeur (Tel 01 65 84 46 88, rifugioelena@virgilio.it) – 128d, 15b: June–Sept

SWITZERLAND

Alpage de la Peule, Val Ferret (Tel 027 783 10 44, coppey.lapeule@dransnet.ch; www.lapeulaz.skyrock.com) – 30pl. open in summer

Hotel Col de Fenêtre, Ferret, 1944 La Fouly (Tel 027 783 11 88, Bertrandmurisier@bluewin.ch) – 18d, 17b: June–Sept

Gîte de la Léchère, Val Ferret, Case postale 373, 1944 La Fouly (Tel 079 433 49 78, www.lalechere.ch) – 35d: June–Sept

LA FOULY

Office de Tourisme, 1944 La Fouly (Tel 027 775 23 84; www.lafouly.ch/en)

Chalet Le Dolent, 1944 La Fouly (Tel 027 783 29 31, info@dolent.ch; www.dolent. ch) – 65d,10b: all year

Gîte les Girolles, 1944 La Fouly (Tel 027 783 18 75, lesgirolles@netplus.ch) – 60b: all year

Auberge des Glaciers, 1944 La Fouly (Tel 027 783 11 71, info@aubergedesglaciers.ch) – 34d, 22b: June–Oct

Hotel Edelweiss, 1944 La Fouly (Tel 027 783 26 21, hotel.edelweiss@st-bernard.ch) – 25d, 45b: end May–end Sept

CHAMPEX

Office de Tourisme, 1938 Champex-Lac (Tel 027 775 23 83, champexlac@saint-bernard.ch; www.champex.info)

Pension En Plein Air, 1938 Champex-Lac (Tel 027 783 23 50, pensionenplein-air@bluewin.ch) – 48d, 25b: all year

Au Club Alpin, 1938 Champex-Lac (Tel 027 783 11 61) – 25d: all year

Chalet du Jardin Alpin, 1938 Champex-Lac (Tel 027 783 12 17, info@flore-alpe.ch, www.flore-alpe.ch) – 8d, 13b: May–end Oct

Hotel-Club Sunways, Champex d'en Haut (Tel 027 783 11 22) – 77b: Dec–April, June–Sept

Chalet Bon-Abri, Champex d'En Haut (Tel 027 783 14 23, contact@gite-bonabri.com) – 33d, 42b: all year

Hotel du Col de la Forclaz, Col de la Forclaz, 1920 Martigny (Tel 027 722 26 88, colforclazhotel@bluewin.ch; www.coldelaforclaz.ch) – 40d, 35b: mid-Dec–Nov

Relais d'Arpette, 1938 Champex-Lac (Tel 027 783 12 21, info@arpette.ch, www.arpette.ch) – 86d, 14b: May–end Oct

Refuge les Grands (reservations: Tel 026 660 65 04) – 15d: mid-June–mid-Oct

TRIENT

Refuge Du Peuty, Le Peuty, 1929 Trient (Tel 027 722 09 38) – 37d: mid-June–mid-Sept

Auberge Mont Blanc, 1929 Trient (Tel 027 767 15 05, info@aubergemontblanc.com, www.aubergemontblanc.com) – 60d, 20b: all year

La Grande Ourse, 1929 Trient (Tel 027 722 17 54, contact@la-grande-ourse.ch, www.la-grande-ourse.ch) – 38d, 18b, + apartments: all year

FRANCE

Refuge du Col de Balme (Tel 04 50 54 02 33) – 26d: open in summer

TRÉ-LE-CHAMP

Auberge la Boerne, 288 Trélechamps, 74400 Argentière (Tel 04 50 54 05 14, contact@la-boerne.fr; www.la-boerne.fr) – 32d: all year

Gîte le Moulin, 32 Chemin du Moulin, Les Frasserands, 74400 Argentière (Tel 04 50 54 05 37, benoit.henry2@wanadoo.fr, www.gite-chamonix.com) – 38d: Dec–end Sept

LE TOUR

Gîte d'Alpage, Charamillon, Le Tour, 74400 Argentière (Tel 04 50 54 17 07) – 20d: mid-June–mid-Sept

Chalet Alpin du Tour (CAF), Chemin du Rocher Nay, Le Tour, 74400 Argentière (Tel 04 50 54 04 16) – 87d: April–mid-Sept

LE BRÉVENT

Refuge La Flégère, 18 Allée Louis Lachenal, 74400 Chamonix (Tel 06 03 58 28 14, bellay.catherone@wanadoo.fr) – 66d, 21b: mid-June–mid-Sept

Refuge du Lac Blanc, 74400 Les Praz de Chamonix (Tel 04 50 53 49 14) – 40d: mid-June–end Sept

Refuge de Bellachat, 305 Route de Vers le Nant, 74400 Chamonix (Tel 04 50 53 43 23, Refuge: 07 89 03 30 38, www.refuge-bellachat.com/refuge) – 28d: late June–mid-Sept

APPENDIX B
Useful contacts

Tourist Information
French Government Tourist Office
178 Piccadilly
London W1J 9AL
Tel 0906 8244123 (60p/min)
info.uk@franceguide.com
www.franceguide.com

Italian State Tourist Board
1 Princes Street
London W1B 2AY
Tel 020 7408 1254
www.enit.it
www.italiantouristboard.co.uk

Switzerland Travel Centre Ltd
30 Bedford Street
London WC2E 9ED
Tel 0207 420 4900
sales@stc.co.uk
www.stc.co.uk

British Mountaineering Council
177–179 Burton Road
Manchester M20 2BB
Tel 0870 010 4878
office@thebmc.co.uk
www.thebmc.co.uk

Club Alpin Français (CAF)
136 av. Michel Croz
74400 Chamonix, France
Tel 04 50 53 16 03
www.clubalpin-chamonix.com

Club Alpino Italiano (CAI)
Via Errico Petrella 19
C.P. 17106
20124 Milano, Italy
www.cai.it

Club Alpin Suisse (CAS)
Monbijou str. 61
CH-3000 Berne, Switzerland
www.sac-cas.ch

Map Suppliers
Edward Stanford Ltd
12–14 Long Acre
London WC2E 9LP
sales@stanfords.co.uk
www.stanfords.co.uk

The Map Shop
15 High Street
Upton-upon-Severn
Worcs WR8 0HJ
themapshop@btinternet.com
www.themapshop.co.uk

Cordee
charlie@cordee.co.uk
www.cordee.co.uk

Rand McNally Map Store
10 East 53rd Street
New York
NY, US

Omni Resources
PO Box 2096
1004 South Mebane Street
Burlington
NC 27216-2096, US
custserv@omnimap.com
www.omnimap.com/maps.htm

ITMB
345 West Broadway
Vancouver, BC
V5Y 1PB, Canada
Tel 604 879 3621

Map Link Inc
30 South La Patera Lane
Unit 5
Santa Barbara
California 93117, US

Specialist Mountain Activities Insurers
(AAC members only)
Austrian Alpine Club
Unit 43
Glenmore Business Park
Blackhill Road
Holton Heath
Poole
Dorset BH16 6NL
aac.office@aacuk.org.uk
www.aacuk.org.uk
*(membership carries automatic
accident and rescue insurance)*

BMC Travel and Activity Insurance
177–179 Burton Road
Manchester M20 2BB
Tel 0870 010 4878
www.thebmc.co.uk
(BMC members only)

Harrison Beaumont Ltd
Unit 3, Meridian Office Park
Osborn Way
Hook
Hampshire RG27 9HY
Tel 0844 875 3506
info@hbinsurance.co.uk
www.hbinsurance.co.uk

Snowcard Insurance Services
308–314 London Road
Hadleigh
Essex SS7 2DD
Tel 0844 826 2699
www.snowcard.co.uk

Organised Treks Round the TMB
Alpine Exploratory Ltd
7 Victoria Street
Settle BD24 9HD
Tel 01729 823 197
www.alpineexploratory.com

Exodus Travels Ltd
Grange Mills
Weir Road
London SW12 0NE
Tel 0845 004 8272
info@exodus.co.uk
www.exodus.co.uk

Mountain Kingdoms Ltd
20 Long Street
Wotton-under-Edge
Glos GL12 7BT
Tel 01453 844400
info@mountainkingdoms.com
www.mountainkingdoms.com

Ramblers Holidays
Lemsford Mill
Lemsford Village
Welwyn Garden City
AL8 7TR
Tel 01707 331133
info@ramblersholidays.co.uk
www.ramblersholidays.co.uk

Sherpa Expeditions
81 Craven Gardens
Wimbledon
London SW19 8LU
Tel 020 8577 2717
sales@sherpa-walking-holidays.co.uk
www.sherpaexpeditions.com

Trekking in the Alps
Le Village
26510 Villeperdrix
France
Tel 0033 6 8265 4214
www.trekkinginthealps.com

APPENDIX C
Further reading

The mountaineering library contains literally hundreds of volumes devoted to Mont Blanc, the number of which increases year by year. The following list is by necessity a very selective one.

General Tourist Guides

Michelin Green Guide: French Alps (Michelin, Watford 1998) – Standard tourist guide covering the French Alps from Mont Blanc to the Alpes Maritime, with basic information regarding Chamonix, Les Houches, Les Contamines, etc.

Mont Blanc and the Seven Valleys by Roger Frison-Roche (Nicholas Kaye, London 1961) – The English translation of a beautifully illustrated volume originally published in France. With 170 magnificent b&w photographs by Pierre Tairraz, Frison-Roche's book follows the route of the TMB and describes the mountain and each of the valleys in turn. Long out of print, but worth searching for.

The Alps by RLG Irving (Batsford, London 1939) – Also long out of print, but may be available by special order from public libraries or via internet booksearch sites, this book contains lengthy passages of interest to anyone tackling the TMB. Irving was a noted alpine connoisseur and climber, a Winchester schoolmaster whose most famous pupil was George Mallory, who died on Everest in 1924.

The Outdoor Traveler's Guide to the Alps by Marcia R Lieberman (Stewart, Tabori & Chang, New York 1991) – Much of the Alpine chain is described by a noted American author, albeit in brief essays. The Mont Blanc range is of course included. The book is illustrated by Tim Thompson's quality colour photographs.

Mont Blanc for the Mountaineer

Alps 4000 by Martin Moran (David & Charles, Devon 1994) – The fascinating account of Moran's and Simon Jenkins's epic journey across all the 4000m summits of the Alps in one summer's frenetic activity.

Between Heaven and Earth by Gaston Rébuffat (Nicholas Vane, London 1962) – Photography and text from an award-winning film which describes the life of a professional guide, mostly shot around the Mont Blanc massif. Illustrated by the master of Mont Blanc photography, Pierre Tairraz.

Mont Blanc and the Aiguilles by C Douglas Milner (Robert Hale, London 1955) – Milner's book looks at the history of climbing in the Mont Blanc range, and is illustrated with several photographs that will be of interest to TMB walkers.

Mont Blanc Massif – Vols I & II by Lindsay Griffin (Alpine Club, London 1991) – A two-volume series of climbing guides to selected routes by that doyen of mountaineering journalists.

Mountaineering in the Alps by Claire Elaine Engel (Allen & Unwin, London 1971) – An historical survey which has a heavy concentration on Mont Blanc and the characters involved in mountaineering there.

Savage Snows by Walt Unsworth (Hodder & Stoughton, London 1986) – A highly readable selective history of Mont Blanc which picks out the highlights of its first 200 years. Authoritative and entertaining, and highly recommended.

Scrambles Amongst the Alps by Edward Whymper (first edition 1871, numerous editions since, it's almost always in print) – Best-known for the story of the tragic first ascent of the Matterhorn, this splendid book also recounts Whymper's climbs in the Mont Blanc range. A much-respected volume, recommended to all would-be mountaineers.

The High Mountains of the Alps by Helmut Dumler and Willi P Burkhardt (Diadem, London 1994) – Sumptuously illustrated in colour throughout, this large-format volume is more than a 'coffee-table book', for it has an intelligent text which describes all the Alpine 4000m peaks, including those of the Mont Blanc range.

The Mont Blanc Massif – The 100 finest routes by Gaston Rébuffat (Kaye & Ward, London 1974) – The ultimate list-ticker's selection of climbs by the late well-known guide and author. Even if you're not a climber the book is worth having for the evocative photographs by Pierre Tairraz.

The Mountains of Europe by Kev Reynolds (Oxford Illustrated Press, Sparkford 1990) – In this book the Mont Blanc range is described by C Douglas Milner, a noted authority on the massif.

Walking Guides

Mont Blanc Walks by Hilary Sharp (Cicerone Press, Milnthorpe 2005) – A selection of 50 walks and 4 multi-day treks on both the French and Italian sides of Mont Blanc by the Vallorcine-based author and trek leader. A good introduction for anyone planning a centre-based holiday there.

Chamonix Valley by Terry Marsh (Inghams Hotelplan, London 1998) – One of a series of walking guides produced for Inghams, this has 20 walks of varying lengths and degrees of difficulty described and illustrated by a well-known author. Only available to guests of Inghams holidays.

Classic Walks in the Alps by Kev Reynolds (Oxford Illustrated Press, Sparkford 1991) – This large-format hardback naturally includes a chapter on the TMB written by Andrew Harper, author of the first English-language guide to the route.

Classic Walks of the World by Walt Unsworth (Oxford Illustrated Press, Sparkford 1985) – One of the first in a long series of Classic Walks collections (see above), this volume rightly includes the Tour of Mont Blanc.

Tour du Mont Blanc (FFRP, Paris) – This regularly updated *topoguide* describes the route in brief paragraphs of French text accompanied by extracts of IGN mapping.

Trekking in the Alps edited by Kev Reynolds (Cicerone Press, Milnthorpe 2011) – A sumptuously illustrated celebration of 20 of the finest multi-day tours in the Alps, including the TMB.

Walking in the Alps by Kev Reynolds (Cicerone Press, Milnthorpe 2nd ed 2005) – From the Alpes Maritime to the Julian Alps of Slovenia, this 500pp tome describes walking possibilities in 19 different regions. The TMB is covered, plus day-walk options in the area.

Walking in the Alps by Helen Fairburn et al (Lonely Planet, London 2004) – The Tour of Mont Blanc is included in this selection of multi-day routes in various Alpine regions.

100 Hut Walks in the Alps by Kev Reynolds (Cicerone Press, Milnthorpe 3rd edn 2014) – As the title suggests, a large selection of routes to mountain huts across the Alpine chain. Several refuges visited by the TMB are included.

Aquarelles sur le Tour du Mont Blanc by Marie-Paule Roc (Libris, Grenoble 2005) – A charming series of watercolours made during a trek around the TMB, with brief French and English captions. The book makes an evocative souvenir, and is on sale in Chamonix bookshops.

Alpine Points of View by Kev Reynolds (Cicerone Press, Milnthorpe 2004) – A collection of 101 full-page colour photographs, plus text, illustrating the rich diversity of Europe's premier mountain range from the walker's viewpoint. Several of the photos were taken along the TMB.

Explore the Tour of Mont Blanc by Gareth McCormack (Rucksack Readers, Dunblane 2005) – An all-colour guide to the TMB in spiral-bound format, by one of the authors of the Lonely Planet guide to the Alps (see above).

Trekking & Climbing in the Western Alps by Hilary Sharp (New Holland, London 2002) – Written and illustrated by the author of the Mont Blanc Walks guide, this selection of 22 treks includes the Tour of Mont Blanc.

Walking & Climbing in the Alps by Stefano Ardito (Swan Hill Press, Shrewsbury 1995) – The TMB is one of 18 multi-day routes described in this large-format hardback.

Tour du Mont Blanc by Jim Manthorpe (Trailblazer, 2008) – A recent addition to the list of TMB guides, it describes the route in an anti-clockwise direction.

APPENDIX D
French–English Glossary

FRENCH	ENGLISH
abri	shelter
accompagnateur	walking guide
aigle	eagle
aiguille	sharp peak or needle
alimentation	grocery store
aller-retour	round-trip, there and back
alpage	alpine meadow
alpiniste	mountaineer
ampoule	blister
arête	ridge
arrêt autocar	bus stop
auberge	inn, guesthouse
auberge de jeunesse	youth hostel
autobus	bus
bain	bath
balisage	waymark
banque	bank
barrage	dam
bas	lower, below
batons	trekking poles
beau temps	good weather
bellevue	literally 'good view' viewpoint
bergerie	shepherd's hut
bière	beer
bière pression	draft beer
blanc	white
bois	woodland
boucherie	butcher's shop
boulangerie	bakery
bouquetin	ibex
brouillard	fog, mist
buvette	snack bar or café
cairn	cairn
carte	map

FRENCH	ENGLISH
chalet-refuge	mountain inn
chambre	bedroom
chambre d'hôte	b&b
chaud	warm
chausseurs de montagne	boots
chemin	way, or road
chemin de fer	railway
chemin pédestre	footpath
chute de pierres	stonefall
club alpin	alpine club
col	pass
colline	hill
combe	cwm, small valley
complet	full (accommodation)
corde	rope
couchette	bunk bed
couloir	steep gully
coup de soleil	sunstroke
crête	crest, ridge
croix	cross
dangereux	dangerous
défense de	forbidden
déjeuner	lunch
demi-pension	half-board (b&b and evening meal)
dent	tooth
dépôt de pain	shop selling bread
dessous	under, lower
dessus	upper
diner	dinner
dortoir	dormitory
douche	shower
droit	right (direction)
eau	water
éboulis	scree

FRENCH	ENGLISH	FRENCH	ENGLISH
echange	exchange (currency)	occupé	occupied (toilet)
éclair	lightning	office du tourisme	tourist office
église	church	orage	storm
est	east	ouest	west
facile	easy	ouvert	open
fermé	closed	pain	bread
forêt	forest	passerelle	footbridge
fourche	fork	pâturage	pasture
froid	cold	pension	boarding house
gardien	hut-keeper/refuge warden	complète	full board
gare	railway station	pharmacie	chemist
garni	b&b hotel	piolet	ice axe
gauche	left (direction)	plan	plain, plateau, flat area
géant	giant, huge	pluie	rain
gîte d'étape	privately-owned hostel-style accommodation	pont	bridge
glace	ice	raccourci	shortcut
grange	barn	randonnée	walk or hike
grimpeur	mountain walker	randonneur	hiker, rambler
hameau	hamlet	rappel	rope down (abseil); reminder
hébergement	accommodation	refuge	mountain hut
heure	hour	renseignements	information
horaire	timetable	rivière	river
lac	lake	route	road
lacets	zigzags	routière	bus station
libre	free	réservoir	reservoir
logement	accommodation	ruisseau	stream
magasin	shop	sac à dos	rucksack
marmotte	marmot	sac à viande	sheet sleeping bag
maudit	cursed	sac de couchage	sleeping bag
mauvais	bad; poor	secours	help
météo	weather forecast	secours en montagne	mountain rescue
montagne	mountain	sentier	footpath
moulin	mill	soleil	sunny
navette	shuttle (bus)	sommet	summit
neige	snow	source	spring (water)
névé	field of old snow	souterrain	underground
nord	north	sud	south
nuage (nuageaux)	cloud (cloudy)	supermarché	supermarket
		syndicat d'initiative	tourist office

FRENCH	ENGLISH
télécarte	telephone card
téléphérique	cablecar
télésiège	chairlift
tempête	storm
terrain de camping	campsite
tête	head, summit
tonnerre	thunder
tour	tour; tower
torrent	mountain stream
tronçon	section
usine hydro electrique	hydro-electric works
val, vallée, vallon,	
vallee	valley
vélo tout terrain/VTT	mountain bike
vent	wind

Menu items

FRENCH	ENGLISH
ail	garlic
casse-croûte	snack
chips	crisps
crevettes	shrimps
croque madame	toasted ham and cheese sandwich, with egg
croque monsieur	as above, but without the egg
croute au fromage	hot cheese and garlic bread
fondue	bubbling hot cheese, with diced bread to dip
frites	French fries/chips
fromage	cheese
jambon	ham (boiled)
jambon cru	raw sliced ham
jambon fumé	smoked ham
lardon	cubes of bacon
omelette natur	plain omelette
oeuf	egg
pommes	apples
pommes de terre	potatoes
raclette	melted cheese, served with small boiled potatoes
rösti	fried grated potato with onion and bacon
thé	tea
thé au lait	tea with milk
thon	tuna
tisane	herb tea

LISTING OF CICERONE GUIDES

SCOTLAND
Backpacker's Britain:
   Northern Scotland
Ben Nevis and Glen Coe
Cycling in the Hebrides
Great Mountain Days in Scotland
Mountain Biking in Southern and
   Central Scotland
Mountain Biking in West and
   North West Scotland
Not the West Highland Way
Scotland
Scotland's Best Small Mountains
Scotland's Far West
Scotland's Mountain Ridges
Scrambles in Lochaber
The Ayrshire and Arran
   Coastal Paths
The Border Country
The Cape Wrath Trail
The Great Glen Way
The Great Glen Way Map Booklet
The Hebridean Way
The Hebrides
The Isle of Mull
The Isle of Skye
The Skye Trail
The Southern Upland Way
The Speyside Way
The Speyside Way Map Booklet
The West Highland Way
Walking Highland Perthshire
Walking in Scotland's Far North
Walking in the Angus Glens
Walking in the Cairngorms
Walking in the Ochils, Campsie
   Fells and Lomond Hills
Walking in the Pentland Hills
Walking in the Southern Uplands
Walking in Torridon
Walking Loch Lomond and
   the Trossachs
Walking on Arran
Walking on Harris and Lewis
Walking on Jura, Islay
   and Colonsay
Walking on Rum and the
   Small Isles
Walking on the Orkney and
   Shetland Isles
Walking on Uist and Barra
Walking the Corbetts
   Vol 1 South of the Great Glen
Walking the Corbetts
   Vol 2 North of the Great Glen
Walking the Galloway Hills

Walking the Munros
   Vol 1 – Southern, Central and
   Western Highlands
Walking the Munros
   Vol 2 – Northern Highlands
   and the Cairngorms
West Highland Way Map Booklet
Winter Climbs Ben Nevis and
   Glen Coe
Winter Climbs in the Cairngorms

NORTHERN ENGLAND TRAILS
Hadrian's Wall Path
Hadrian's Wall Path Map Booklet
Pennine Way Map Booklet
The Coast to Coast Map Booklet
The Coast to Coast Walk
The Dales Way
The Pennine Way

LAKE DISTRICT
Cycling in the Lake District
Great Mountain Days in the
   Lake District
Lake District Winter Climbs
Lake District: High Level and
   Fell Walks
Lake District: Low Level and
   Lake Walks
Lakeland Fellranger series
Mountain Biking in the
   Lake District
Scrambles in the
   Lake District – North
Scrambles in the
   Lake District – South
Short Walks in Lakeland
   Books 1, 2 and 3
The Cumbria Coastal Way
The Cumbria Way
Tour of the Lake District
Trail and Fell Running in the
   Lake District

NORTH WEST ENGLAND AND THE ISLE OF MAN
Cycling the Pennine Bridleway
Isle of Man Coastal Path
The Lancashire Cycleway
The Lune Valley and Howgills – A
   Walking Guide
The Ribble Way
Walking in Cumbria's Eden Valley
Walking in Lancashire
Walking in the Forest of Bowland
   and Pendle
Walking on the Isle of Man

Walking on the West
   Pennine Moors
Walks in Lancashire
   Witch Country
Walks in Ribble Country
Walks in Silverdale and Arnside
Walks in the Forest of Bowland

NORTH EAST ENGLAND, YORKSHIRE DALES AND PENNINES
Cycling in the Yorkshire Dales
Great Mountain Days in
   the Pennines
Historic Walks in North Yorkshire
Mountain Biking in the
   Yorkshire Dales
South Pennine Walks
St Oswald's Way and
   St Cuthbert's Way
The Cleveland Way and the
   Yorkshire Wolds Way
The Cleveland Way Map Booklet
The North York Moors
The Reivers Way
The Teesdale Way
Walking in County Durham
Walking in Northumberland
Walking in the North Pennines
Walking in the Yorkshire Dales:
   North and East
Walking in the Yorkshire Dales:
   South and West
Walks in Dales Country
Walks in the Yorkshire Dales

WALES AND WELSH BORDERS
Glyndwr's Way
Great Mountain Days
   in Snowdonia
Hillwalking in Shropshire
Hillwalking in Wales – Vol 1
Hillwalking in Wales – Vol 2
Mountain Walking in Snowdonia
Offa's Dyke Path
Offa's Dyke Map Booklet
Pembrokeshire Coast Path
   Map Booklet
Ridges of Snowdonia
Scrambles in Snowdonia
The Ascent of Snowdon
The Ceredigion and Snowdonia
   Coast Paths
The Pembrokeshire Coast Path
The Severn Way
The Snowdonia Way

For full information on all our
guides, books and eBooks,
visit our website:
www.cicerone.co.uk

Walking – Trekking – Mountaineering – Climbing – Cycling

Over 40 years, Cicerone have built up an outstanding collection of over 300 guides, inspiring all sorts of amazing adventures.

Every guide comes from extensive exploration and research by our expert authors, all with a passion for their subjects. They are frequently praised, endorsed and used by clubs, instructors and outdoor organisations.

All our titles can now be bought as **e-books**, **ePubs** and **Kindle** files and we also have an online magazine – **Cicerone Extra** – with features to help cyclists, climbers, walkers and trekkers choose their next adventure, at home or abroad.

Our website shows any **new information** we've had in since a book was published. Please do let us know if you find anything has changed, so that we can publish the latest details. On our **website** you'll also find great ideas and lots of detailed information about what's inside every guide and you can buy **individual routes** from many of them online.

It's easy to keep in touch with what's going on at Cicerone by getting our monthly **free e-newsletter**, which is full of offers, competitions, up-to-date information and topical articles. You can subscribe on our home page and also follow us on Facebook and Twitter or dip into our **blog**.

Cicerone – the very best guides for exploring the world.

CICERONE

Juniper House, Murley Moss, Oxenholme Road, Kendal, Cumbria LA9 7RL
Tel: 015395 62069 info@cicerone.co.uk
www.cicerone.co.uk and **www.cicerone-extra.com**